Behold a white horse!

*And
its rider
had a bow,*

*And a crown
was given to him,*

*And
he
went out conquering
to conquer.*

*And
the armies of heaven,
followed him
on white horses,*

*They
arrayed in fine linen
white and pure.*

Rev 6:2, 19:11,14

White Horse = Heavenly Power
Rider = Second Coming of the Messiah
Armies = Those on the Messiah's Way

Jesus' Way Of Wisdom

Volume One

How 53 of Jesus' Poems Decoded
In the Gospel of Thomas
Reveal His Unknown, Revolutionary Good News
And How and Why the Apostle Paul Altered It

By

Robert W. North

Way of Wisdom
www.7771.org

Jesus' Way Of Wisdom

Volume One

How 53 of Jesus' Poems Decoded
In the Gospel of Thomas
Reveal His Unknown, Revolutionary Good News
And How and Why the Apostle Paul Altered It

Copyright © 2014 by Robert W. North

All rights reserved. No part of this book may be used or reproduced by any means, graphic, electronic, or mechanical, including photocopying, recording, taping or by any information storage retrieval system without the written permission of the publisher except in the case of brief quotations embodied in critical articles and reviews.

To Contact the Author
www.7771.Org

Because of the dynamic nature of the Internet, any Web addresses or links contained in this book may have changed since publication and may no longer be valid.

ISBN-13: 978-0-9907795-7-5

Way of Wisdom
www.7771.org

TABLE OF CONTENTS

Preface — vii
- Jesus' Good-news — ix
- The Apostle Paul's Mission — x
- The Messiah's Mission — xi
- The Good-news as a Paradigm-shift — xi
- Jesus' Problem — xiii
- The Gospel of Thomas — xiv
- The Organization of Semitic Books — xiv
- This Author's Journey — xv

Foreword — xix
- Future Volumes — xx

Introduction — xxi
- Jesus' Legacy — xxi
- The Two Ways — xxi
- The Way of Religion — xxii
- The Inherent Conflicts on the Way of Religion — xxiii
- The Way of Wisdom — xviv
- The Mission of the Messiah — xv

Chapter One: The Gospel of Thomas — 1
- The Gospel of Thomas and the New Testament? — 1
- Does the Gospel of Thomas Contain Jesus' Gospel? — 1
- Background — 2
- The Nag Hammadi Discovery — 2
- The Gospel of Thomas — 5
- Semitic Parallelism and the Organization of Thomas — 9
- The Organization of Books of the Bible — 10
- Suggestions — 11

Chapter Two: Jesus' Gospel: Become Fully Human — 13
- The Two Means of Knowing — 13
- Become a Kingdom — 14
- The Soul-Knowing Process — 16
- The World — 27

Discover Rather than Believe	30
Become Like a Little child	32
Distinguish Between Light and Darkness in People	40
Recognize Our Two Mothers	52
Become the All	55

Chapter Three: Paul's View of The Human Condition — 59

Paul Rejects Jesus' Way	59
Paul's View of a Little Child	61
Jesus' and Man's Body	62
Paul's Belief in the Unseen	63

Chapter Four: The Goals of Jesus' Way of Wisdom — 65

Discover the Kingdom	65
Will of the Father	68
Hate your Father and Mother?	70
Leave Your Sexual Identity	71
Evolve Through Heavens	73
Evolve to Know Your Divinity	79
Be a Twin	82
Be a Lion	84
Love-Guard	88
Be Cunning and Innocent	92
Summary	96

Chapter Five: Paul's Goals — 97

Blot Out Jesus' Gospel	98
Declare that Jesus is God	99
Declare that Jesus Died for Humankind's Sins	101
Declare that People Need to Believe Paul's Gospel	103
Declare that Jesus was the Messiah	104
Found a Religion to Indoctrinate People	104

Chapter Six: Jesus' Self-Development Method — 107

Discover Yourself on Your Own	107
Make the Right Fundamental Choice	108
LoveGuard Indoctrinators	112
Master Your Fields	121
Seek to Destroy Yourself	129
Destroy Your Divided Self	131
Get Lost	134
Become in the Beginning	136

"Our end will come in what manner?"	137
Seek and Find	152
Jesus' Five Steps to Sanity and Fulfillment	161

Chapter Seven: Paul's Self-Development Method — 163

Be Saved by Your Faith in Paul's Gospel	163
Avoid Evil Deeds	164
Obey Paul's Laws	164
Do Good	166
Indoctrinate Non-Believers	169

Chapter Eight: The Results of Living Jesus' Way of Wisdom — 173

Introduction	173
A Mountain	175
A Kingdom	178
A Twin	180
An Empty One	183
Invulnerability	185
A Child and a Lion	187

Chapter Nine: The Results of Living Paul's Way of Religion — 189

Salvation and Righteousness	189
Trouble and Distress	190
Inherit the Kingdom	191

Chapter Ten: Conclusions — 195

What We Know About the Author of Thomas	195
Who Authored the Gospel of Thomas?	199
What Do We Know About the Messiah?	199
The Priest and King Traditions in the Bible	200
The Role of the Priest Messiah	206
The Role of the King Messiah	208
Was Jesus the Messiah?	212

Acknowledgements — 215

PREFACE

Jesus' Good-news

The word, "gospel" means "good-news." In the Gospel of Mark (1:14), we read: "Jesus came into Galilee preaching the gospel (good-news) of God. Matthew in his Gospel (4:23) explains that Jesus "went about all Galilee teaching in their synagogues and preaching the gospel (good-news) of the kingdom. Luke in his Gospel (20:1) states that "he (Jesus) was teaching the people in the temple and preaching the gospel (good-news)."

Mark tells us that Jesus preached the "good-news of God." Matthew calls Jesus' message and mission, "the good-news of the kingdom." So, the good news involves establishing a "kingdom" that is God's way of living. How does one follow that "way?"

Matthew, Mark and Luke never concisely answer those questions. Strangely, no one else, to my knowledge, knows the answers.

Some say that Jesus' good-news can be found in Jesus' statements such as, "Blessed are the poor in spirit, for theirs is the kingdom of heaven" (Matt 5:3). However, there is no consensus about what the phrase "poor in spirit" means and how that could be connected to a "kingdom."

"Some say the Jesus intended to found a physical "kingdom." If so, he failed. Others think that he was teaching people to live an inner kind of "kingdom" life; however, no one seems to know exactly how to live it.

Some say that Jesus' good-news was that we are saved when we believe:

- That Adam and Eve committed an "original sin" and that it is passed down to all of humankind spiritually,

- That Jesus was the son of God in a way that we are not,
- That Jesus sacrificed himself on the cross to free us from original sin,
- That he rose from the dead, and
- That he will come again to judge the living and the dead.

However, *Jesus never said those things*; the Apostle Paul was inspired to preach that interpretation of Jesus' good-news *10 years after Jesus died.*

Some say that we find Jesus' good-news in the Nicene Creed that people recite at Christian services as the foundation of their faith. However, it can be argued that Jesus did not utter a single statement in that creed. In fact, Jesus never articulated a creed or preached that one is better in any way by believing in one.

Thus, billions of people in the past 20 centuries have thought that they understood Jesus and his mission to bring us into good-news. Further, most if not all Christians have endured hardship for their understanding of Jesus' good-news. Yet, Christians have not only disagreed on the nature of Jesus' message and for what they were suffering, most never questioned the difference between Paul's and Jesus' gospels.

The Apostle Paul's Mission

Questions: Why did the Apostle Paul choose to never quote Jesus? How could he preach Jesus' good-news without explaining his words? Why did Paul invent his own version of the "good-news" to substitute for that of Jesus? Why have Christian leaders including the great theologians St. Augustine and Thomas Aquinas, and the Popes, Patriarchs and Presidents of Christian sects chosen to adopt Paul's message rather than Jesus'? Indeed, we all might ask, "Would Jesus be a follower of Paul?"

After you finish this book, you will have information that will suggest why.

The Messiah's Mission

The word "Christ" means "Messiah." If Jesus were the Christ, his mission would be to:

1. Bring oneness (fulfillment and joy) to each individual in any situation, and

2. Bring oneness (peace) to the world.

Conclusion: Internal and external *division* is the "bad-news" that Jesus needed to address. (Various forms of the word "division" and "oneness" are frequently used throughout the Gospel of Thomas; thus, they are key to understanding the main theme).

Therefore, either Jesus was not the promised Messiah that would preach unifying "good-news," or no one ever understood him, or people were so threatened by his solution that they altered it.

The Good-news as a Paradigm-shift

If Jesus articulated and lived good-news, it would be a paradigm-shift in how people divided within themselves and from others generally view and treat themselves and each other. Thus, his unifying "kingdom" would cross all boarders, psychologically, culturally, and geographically.

A paradigm-shift system of ideas constitutes a radical rethinking, and sometimes a radical reliving of the prevailing world-view. When someone presents a paradigm-shift notion, often he is greeted with mockery and his idea ridiculed. Those living the old world-view consider the new one as going against soundly established truths, and sometimes, common sense.

For example, Aristarchus of Samos (310 BCE – 230 BCE) was the first to advance a theory that the earth orbited the sun. That was a paradigm-shift notion that countered what people considered common sense—that the sun rotated around the earth.

For the next 2000 years, this radically different heliocentric system of ideas was discussed and rejected by many prominent philosophers, foremost among them were Aristotle and Ptolemy. In his treatise, *Almagest*, composed circa 150 CE; the latter argued philosophically and mathematically that the earth was the stationary center of the universe. Stars were embedded in a large outer sphere which rotated rapidly, approximately daily, while each of the planets, the sun, and the moon were embedded in their own, smaller spheres.

By the Middle Ages, such ideas took on a new power as the philosophy of Aristotle and Ptolemy and others was wedded to Medieval theology in the great synthesis of Christianity and reason undertaken by philosopher-theologians such as Thomas Aquinas. The Prime Mover of Aristotle's universe became the God of Christian theology. The outer sphere containing the sun and the stars became identified with the Christian Heaven with God controlling it.

Thus, the ideas largely originating with pagan Greek philosophers were baptized into the Christian church and eventually assumed the power of religious dogma: to challenge this view of the universe was not merely a scientific issue; it became a theological one as well, and subjected dissenters to the considerable and not always benevolent power of the Church.

Gradually, great minds such as Copernicus, Kepler, and Galileo risked their reputation and lives to promote the paradigm-shift sun at the center (heliocentric) world-view. It was not until after Isaac Newton formulated the universal law of gravitation and the laws of mechanics in his 1687 Principia was the heliocentric view generally accepted—2000 years after Aristarchus introduced it!

We resist paradigm-shift notions, because to accept them we need to give up what we know and embrace new assumptions and logic. That presents almost insurmountable obstacles for us, because the old world-view gives us meaning. It tells us how to view ourselves, others, God, good and evil, and how to overcome hardship and face death.

Therefore, in order to maintain the old world-view, we ignore and distort contrary evidence and make up blind beliefs that we call "evidence." In short, in order to protect ourselves, we will choose to live in a dream.

Did Jesus introduce into the world a paradigm-shift system of ideas that would bring oneness both to each individual and to conflicting groups in the world? If he did, his followers did not embrace it. If not, he was not the Christ.

Jesus' Problem

If Jesus offered a paradigm-shift system of ideas to bring oneness to individuals and to humankind, we would expect that he would have had few, if any followers. People would have tried to distort what he said to make it compatible with their Jewish/Roman/Greek culture, they would have ridiculed him, and they would have punished, and, even, killed him.

After he died, a charismatic leader who honored Jesus as the Messiah but who disagreed with Jesus' good-news might even have founded another religion that was called "Christianity." That leader, of course, would never quote Jesus, because doing so would have revealed the good-news that would upset the order that gave him meaning. Instead, he would preach an alternative gospel. After 2000 years, we would expect that people belonging to that religion would be so accepting of its version of Jesus' good news that they would not question whether he would endorse it.

Let us suppose that Jesus knew that that would happen; so before he died, he composed a book that would present fully his paradigm-shift world-view. We can expect that after he was murdered, that book would have been misunderstood, hidden, dismissed for many years, and certainly not included in the Bible when the leaders of Christianity compiled the New Testament about 300 years after Jesus died.

The Gospel of Thomas

In 1945, an ancient book was discovered buried in a huge jar in the upper Nile of Egypt. The first sentence states that Jesus was the author. The second one, that he dictated it to his disciple Thomas. On the last page, a scribe scribbled, "The Gospel of Thomas." The book has since been dated to the first or second century. (Was that the original title given to it? Probably not. Early religious documents were usually not given titles).

The Gospel of Thomas is now, perhaps, the most intensively studied ancient Christian document. (A Chapter in this Book will describe in detail the discovery).

The Organization of Semitic Books

I have been studying the Gospel of Thomas fulltime for over 15 years. Other researchers have been using traditional Biblical scholarship tools. Few seemed to have approached it as I have. Permit me to explain that.

Many think that the Books of the Bible were organized into Chapters and verses by their authors. That was not the case. That artificial organization was imposed on the Books for printing purposes in the 13th and 14th century's.

One needs to know the author's true organization to interpret his meaning. Scholars have known for a long time that the Biblical Books contain organizational clues that we have not been able to fully decode. Some have called the rules that the ancient Semitic authors used, "Semitic Parallelism."[1,2]

I was introduced to Semitic Parallelism by William Mountain, S. J. 40 years ago. At that time, scholars were only beginning to discover the ancient ways of composing and reading the text (actually, the Semitic audience primarily did not read the work, they listened to it orally; thus, the rules are for the ear primarily, not for our reading eyes).[3] I became almost obsessed with learning how to decode the books of the Bible.

Over the years, I discovered that much of what Bill Mountain and others taught me was inadequate and sometimes, dead wrong; however, I kept up the search for the secrets to decoding the text. Over 40 years I discovered most of them.

For example, when most read the Bible, they read down columns of text, one after another. They try to understand a word or sentence by studying what came before and after it. Doing it that way tells one practically nothing and misleads.

Many Books of the Bible consist of poems, not straight text. Imagine that Poem One consists of 5 stanzas. Imagine that Poem Two through Five consists of 5 stanzas. So you are looking at a 5 X 5 matrix. Now, instead of reading down one column after another, imagine reading horizontally as you read vertically. What you will find is that the first stanzas in each poem are parallel, that is, that they explain each other. A metaphor in Poem One, Stanza Two will not be explained by what came before or after it. It will be defined in the 4 parallel stanzas. In other words, we find the author's *internal dictionary* by reading horizontally.

To read the Books of the Bible and the Gospel of Thomas that way, one needs to know where the poems and their stanzas break, what words go on each line within a stanza, where the chapters begin and end, and how to organize all of that into a meaningful whole Work. The Semitic Parallelism rules that I discovered tell us that.

THIS AUTHOR'S JOURNEY

When I was introduced to the Gospel of Thomas in 1999, I read it differently than most. Over time, I discovered that it consisted of 135 poems, not 114 "sayings." Further, I found that it was a coherently organized document, not a "collection" of sayings as others thought. Upon further investigation, I found that the book contains such an intricate organization that I concluded that only a single person could have composed it.

However, finding the organization was only half the problem. I also needed to use the organization to determine the meaning of each poem, each stanza, and each metaphor. Fortunately, I had the training to do that.

I was a Jesuit, and in that Catholic Order I received a marvelous Humanistic education. Because of that, I saw that many Books of the Bible, including the four New Testament Gospels are allegories, not historical or semi-historical documents. They consist of a type of Semitic poetry, which one cannot understand without following the Semitic Parallelism rules.

Also, as a Jesuit, I spent two years in intensive philosophical study. We did not use the "objective" philosophical approach, but the experiential, or more technically, a method called, "phenomenology." I later discovered that that is the method employed by most of the Biblical authors, even the authors of Genesis.

After leaving the Order, I studied at the University of Florida under two brilliant phenomenological psychologists: Arthur Combs and Sidney Jourard. That training was perfect for understanding the Bible. Most of the Biblical authors, including the author of the Gospel of Thomas were experiential therapists primarily, not theologians or historians. They did not separate personal growth from spiritual development.

The Gospel of Thomas, for example, contains a coherent method for understanding and addressing mental health. In it is a theory of personality, of motivation, and of how to become a whole, fulfilled person without living the roller coaster life of frustrations, anxiety, worries and regrets alternating with joyful highs that we call "normal." However, to read it, one needs to be able to read poetry and allegories, understand the Semitic

Parallelism rules that lead to decoding the meaning of the metaphors, and have a background in personal development. (I earned a Ph.D. in Counseling from the University of Florida and I have taught therapists).

Endnotes

[1] William Reuben Farmer, *The Synoptic Problem: A Critical Analysis*, Mercer University Press, 1976, p. 253.

[2] Dennis Pardée, *Ugaritic and Hebrew Poetic Parallelism, A Trial Cut*, Brill, 1988, P. 181

[3] Paul J. Achtemeier, "Omne verbum sonat: The New Testament and the Oral Environment of Late Western Antiquity." Journal of Biblical Literature 109, 1 (Spring 1990): 3-27.

FOREWORD

Volume One: This Book is the first of a Series explaining Jesus' good-news. In it you will discover:

- In the Introduction, Jesus' unknown, core insight that explains his understanding of the difference between "bad-news" and "good-news,"

- The hidden meaning of 53 of Jesus' wisdom poems from the Gospel of Thomas,

- How and why the Apostle Paul probably replaced Jesus' good-news with his own,

- How to evolve as a fulfilled person, both spiritually and personally (Again, Jesus did not separate the two), and

- How Jesus' good-news will save the world.

Volume Two: In it you will:

- Learn the Semitic Parallelism rules that I discovered for properly organizing and understanding Biblical Works,

- See how those rules apply to sections of Genesis and the Gospels of Mark, Luke and Thomas,

- Understand how Mark understood and presented Jesus' good-news in an allegorical Gospel,

- Understand how Luke in his allegorical Gospel presented Paul's and not Jesus' good-news,

- See the overall coherent organization of the Gospel of Thomas, and

- Examine the evidence that Jesus composed the Gospel of Thomas.

Future Volumes

I have drafted more books that will be published soon. In them I:

- Explore in detail the organization of each of Jesus' Poems and apply that information to understanding their meaning,

- Present the true organization and meaning of the Garden of Eden Allegory, and

- Provide a guide to living Jesus' Way of Wisdom, that is, how to leave "bad-news" and find a fulfilled life by living his "good-news."

INTRODUCTION

Jesus' Legacy

Jesus came on the scene suddenly, like many other Messiah figures before and since. However, unlike all others, he birthed an unusual legacy. On one hand, many of his followers seek guidance as he did, directly from an outside source of inspiration, that many have called by names like "the Holy Spirit," "God" and "Inner Voice." On the other hand, his followers also subscribe to various doctrines that he did not create.

These doctrines control their actions and thoughts; thus, we find that those affected by Jesus' teachings are torn between independence and dependence, freedom and subservience, and enlightenment and mind control. Out of love for Jesus, many veer from loving and helping everyone, to hating, marginalizing and persecuting those who differ from them in doctrine. In short, most, if not all, of his followers subscribe to both the Way of Wisdom and the Way of Religion.

We find the same phenomenon in many of the followers of Mohammed, the Dalai Lamas, and the Hindu Scriptures. Most in the world are very confused. People want to be independent, but they also want to be controlled by their religions. They want to live fulfilled lives, but they cannot achieve that in a world in which religions cause people to be divided within themselves, and then, again, when they externalize that division in conflicts with others.

The Two Ways

In this book and the next one, I will present evidence that the various authors of the Bible subscribed to one of two opposing

Ways of living: the Way of Religion or the Way of Wisdom. This Introduction will briefly explain the two Ways.

THE WAY OF RELIGION

A person follows a Way of Religion when he identifies with a set of beliefs. These beliefs are a "Way" because they determine how one thinks and acts in relation to himself, others, and the world. They are Ways of "Religion," because when one identifies with a set of beliefs, he defends and promotes them as an extension of himself.

Religions can be secular. For example, one can be "religiously" devoted to his family, his country, his job, his friends, his political party, and even his car. This is because he has developed a set of beliefs centered around those concepts, and comes to identify with them. He sees an attack on them as an attack on himself. He feels pride in himself when they succeed, grow, or gain appreciation. He feels defeated when they fail. He finds kinship in other people who hold the same beliefs that he does.

Everyone subscribes to many Ways of Religion at the same time, be they theological or secular. For example, a Jew may simultaneously belong to Judaism, Zionism, and conservatism. Among these, Judaism is a theological religion, while the others are secular religions. They are all Ways of Religion because those who subscribe to them identify with common doctrines that consist of distinctive beliefs, including values, rules, laws, rituals, traditions, symbols, scriptures, and uniforms.

While the Way of Religion may be a path for the single person; usually single followers band together in social groups. The people on the Way reinforce each other's beliefs, rituals, and rules. Together, they defend their Way against those who disagree with them, and they proselytize to convert others. When they do so, their sense of self is heightened through the group's confidence in their doctrine.

The members of a Way of Religion tend to think that they are independent and free individuals, but in fact, their sense of self is dependent upon the other group members' opinion of how well they conform to the group's doctrine. Therefore, they are not free; others control their thinking and behavior.

All following a Way of Religion seeks to preserve it, because it gives them an identity and establishes meaning for their lives. Consequently, they promote their traditions and beliefs as sacred. They reward people for their steadfast faith, and they build up people who sacrifice or die for their faith.

In order to defend their Way of Religion, adherents often tacitly adopt the notion that the end, survival of their Way, justifies the means. Thus, they may ignore information that does not fit their beliefs, distort information to support their beliefs, ignore outcomes that show that their Way is not beneficial to themselves or society, and blindly believe ideas that are not supported by common sense or experience. They even out of love for their leaders, flag, traditions, buildings, and their doctrine, persecute, marginalize, discriminate against, and even kill people who are threats. In other words, love of me and us justifies hate of others.

The Inherent Conflicts on the Way of Religion

When one identifies with more than one doctrine, he typically encounters some degree of contradiction between them. This causes inner conflict, sometimes called "cognitive dissonance." This can be emotionally painful; therefore, people adopt ways to avoid thinking about ideas, people and events that shine a light on their internal contradictions.

Everyone within every religion has their own lens through which they interpret concepts. Their past experiences, cultures, personality types, etc., form the preexisting framework through which they interpret new ideas. For example, every person who reads the Bible interprets every word and sentence differently.

Therefore, everyone within the same religion eventually comes into ideological conflict. This can result in dysfunction within a group, division between groups, and even ideological schisms that lead to the creation of new religions. Sometimes these conflicts are relatively peaceful, and other times they can be quite violent.

Further, every type of religious group has a fundamental ideological conflict with every other religious group of the same type, because logically, only one doctrine can be true. For example, people from different sects of Christianity come into conflict because of their different beliefs or their different interpretations of the same scriptures.

The Way of Wisdom

When a person *does not identify* with a set of theological or secular beliefs, he follows the Way of Wisdom. Because he does not identify with his doctrine, he does not promote or defend it as an extension of himself. He may argue his opinions; however, because they are not a part of his identity, he can easily modify or give them up entirely. He may argue them to learn their limitations and inaccuracies; however, he neither stands on them for his self-confidence, nor to build himself up over another.

Because a person on the Way of Wisdom does not identify with any doctrines, he is by nature a truth seeker. He does not hold any absolute beliefs. Truth is always something to be discovered. Thus, he never conflicts with others with different beliefs.

The Two Ways Contrasted

Way of Religion		Way of Wisdom
One identifies with his doctrines	→←	One does not identify with any doctrines
One will always be in conflict with himself, because he has an allegiance to many contradictory doctrines	→←	One will not be in conflict with himself
One will always be in conflict with all others of the same faith, because everyone subjectively interprets the common doctrine differently	→←	One will be never be in conflict with others on the Way of Wisdom, because he does not defend or promote any doctrine
One will always be in conflict with others who identify with different doctrines	→←	One will be at peace with everyone

The Mission of the Messiah

Isaiah foretold that the Messiah would establish a kingdom like David's for Jews, then, for the entire world. In Isaiah 9:7 we read:

The abundance
of his rule
will not end.[1]
He
will firmly establish a
throne like David's
over his kingdom[2]
in justice
and in righteousness
from that time on
and forever.

[1] *The abundance of his rule will not end*: Everyone in the world will benefit by the Messiah's rule.

[2] *Kingdom*: David united the Israelites into a kingdom through military power, by the power of his personality, and by establishing a common religion and central place of worship. Thus, Isaiah predicted that the Messiah would do similar things in parallel ways.

David brilliantly united the people of his kingdom around a theological Way of Religion. It created order through laws administered by clerics. It focused everyone on a God, deemed the true and only God; thereby giving people a sense of personal and group superiority over all others. It leveraged their religious devotion into an obedient populace that would sacrifice money, service and their lives in David's army. Ultimately, it gave David and his kingdom power, wealth, territory, peace, and fame.

This is often the short term unifying legacy of a Way of Religion—until it meets another Way of Religion or until the people within it begin to interpret its doctrine differently. Conflict then erupts until one Way becomes dominant. After a short period of peace, another Way of Religion rises to prominence and the cycle begins again. That is the way of the world today.

Because of Isaiah's prophesy and similar ones by other prophets, the Jews of the 1st century awaited the coming of the Messiah that would rule over a worldwide kingdom. This kingdom was expected to both replace the Roman occupation in Palestine and establish a world unifying governance for the peace and prosperity of all. The center of rule and worship would be in Jerusalem in a Temple purified of the worship of false gods, including money and power. The result would be that everyone in the world would respect the Jews and their one, true God as saviors.

Many people have the same dream today—that their Way of Religion will dominate all others and create world peace. Conservatives and liberals dream that; Christians, Muslims, atheists, and skeptics do the same; communists, socialists, capitalists, and nationalists have died for that dream. However, because everyone following any Way of Religion interprets its doctrine differently, they will all eventually find a nightmare of conflict, rather than a promised land of peace and prosperity.

This was as true in 1st century Palestine as it is today. Then, many leaders rose up, claiming to be the expected Messiah. All were quickly killed and their followers scattered. More recently,

Stalin, Hitler, Mao and the Presidents of the United States have come into power declaring that they have the solutions to end conflict. We have seen that the first three were unsuccessful, and the evidence accumulates that a democracy fosters division, lying, corruption, and intransigence internally while it does the same between itself and other governments.

It would seem that the Messiah who would end conflict has not shown up—unless he has and his true message has been hidden.

Was Jesus the Messiah? Did he really preach the gospel to save the world? Through careful analysis of Jesus' wisdom poems, I will enable everyone to decide for themselves whether Jesus taught the Way of Religion or the Way of Wisdom, whether he would support or disrupt most parts of every religion, and whether or not he had the answers that we need today. When we understand the Gospels of Thomas and Mark by following the rules of Semitic Parallelism, we can understand the true message that Jesus taught, and the Way that Jesus lived.

CHAPTER ONE

THE GOSPEL OF THOMAS

THE GOSPEL OF THOMAS AND THE NEW TESTAMENT?

For over 300 years after Jesus died, those who revered him argued about what to include in a New Testament. They could not agree because they each wanted texts that supported their own doctrines. In the 4th century, the leaders of the Church of Peter and Paul (which today is known as the Roman Catholic Church) finally listed the documents we typically find in the New Testament. They were able to make their decision final for others because they had been appointed by Constantine, the Emperor of the Roman Empire to do so.

The Roman Christian Church Bishops based their doctrine on Paul, the Apostle. Logically, those leaders excluded any document antithetical to their creed, such as the Gospel of Thomas. With the backing of Rome, they also ordered both the destruction of documents with competing doctrines and the persecution of people proclaiming them.[1]

DOES THE GOSPEL OF THOMAS CONTAIN JESUS' GOSPEL?

The Gospel of Thomas has not been seen since about 375 C.E. It was discovered in 1945 buried near an ancient Christian monastery in Egypt. In these volumes, you will read the Book as it has not been presented in over 1700 years—as a coherent, highly organized document, probably composed by a single author. You will then possess the evidence to decide three important questions:

1. Does the Gospel of Thomas contain part of the solution for world peace?

2. Is the Messiah the author?

3. Did Jesus compose and dictate the Gospel of Thomas before he died or commission someone who had memorized his compositions to compose it?

Background

In the mid 1940s, the world became aware of two magnificent archeological discoveries. The first occurred in Egypt in 1945 and is known as the "Nag Hammadi Library." These Books are mostly Christian writings composed in the first three centuries CE. The second, better known to laypeople, occurred in 1947, and is known as the "Dead Sea Scrolls." The Dead Sea Scrolls are Jewish writings composed before 70 CE.

The Nag Hammadi Discovery

In December of 1945, in Upper Egypt near the current city of Nag Hammadi (see the map below), two brothers, Muhammad 'Ali and Khalifah, set off on their camels to obtain nitrogen rich soil for use as fertilizer.

Figure 1. *Nag Hammadi in Egypt*

At a large mound called Djebel el Tarif, the brothers began to dig. Soon Muhammad 'Ali unearthed a large, sealed clay pot. Inside he found thirteen leather bound codices filled with crumbling yellowed parchment.

Figure 2. *Area of the Discovery*

Figure 3. *Muhammad 'Ali Who Led the Expedition*

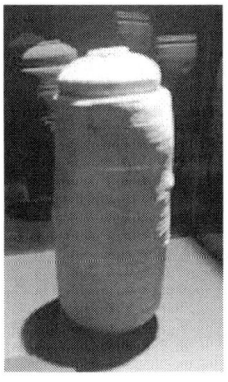

Figure 4. *120 CM High Jar*

Figure 5. *Thirteen Codices*

Figure 6. *A Single Codex Containing Many Books*

Although he was unable to read the text, Muhammad 'Ali knew that the books were ancient and possibly worth a lot of money if sold to antiquities dealers on the black market in Cairo.

What Muhammad 'Ali had discovered was a collection of books that included many Coptic copies of Christian manuscripts composed before 300 CE. Most of the originals seem to have been written in Greek, the language of the New Testament. The buried manuscripts date from the third and fourth centuries.

Muhammad 'Ali took the books to his house. While he was out on an errand, his mother ripped out some of the pages and began to burn the manuscripts as kindling. Fortunately, before all was destroyed, Muhammad 'Ali hid them from her and from the authorities who would confiscate them. He placed them with different friends.

Those friends began to sell them in Cairo. It didn't take long for the books to come to the attention of the Egyptian Department of Antiquities. Over the course of many years, the books were collected and became the property of the state.

While the Dead Sea Scrolls became famous rather quickly, the Nag Hammadi Library was largely unheard of by the general public until the early 1970s. One of the barriers to publication was the absence of scholars who could read and translate Coptic, the language of the documents. The second reason for the hesitant publication was that scholars initially dismissed the documents as arising out of a branch of Christian thinking, called "Gnosticism." They did not believe that Gnosticism contributed much to our understanding of Jesus or early Christianity. Now, many believe the opposite.[2]

THE GOSPEL OF THOMAS

One of the codices contained a Book that scholars today call the "Gospel of Thomas." They gave it that name because a scribe wrote in the last page of the document, "Gospel of Thomas," as shown below in the middle of the page on the left.

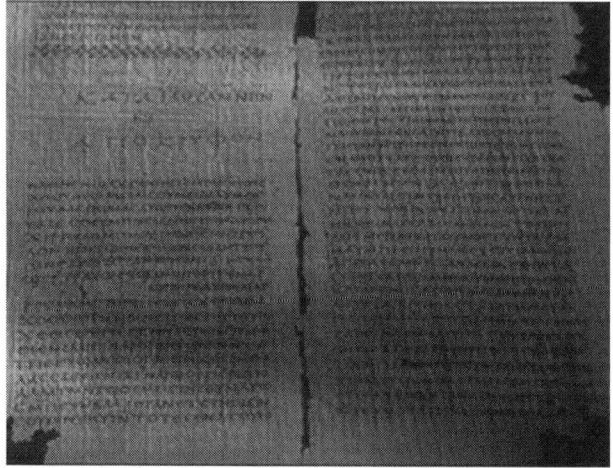

Figure 7. *Two Pages from Coptic Text of the Gospel of Thomas*

The Gospel contains what scholars in the 1950's, shortly after its discovery, considered to be 114 wisdom sayings. In this and the next Volume, I will present evidence that the Gospel contains 135 poems, rather than 114 sayings.

This newly discovered Gospel has become sensational among students of early Christianity. It is studied today not only more than the other Nag Hammadi writings, but also more than any other early Christian document. The reasons are many:

First, Thomas contains in some form about 50% of the parables and sayings that we find in the Gospels of Mark, Luke, Matthew and John. Scholars, therefore, ask, was Thomas composed before or after the New Testament Gospels and by whom?[3]

Some scholars who compare the literary style of the Thomas material find it to be more primitive than those in the New Testament Gospels. For example, the Parable of the Sower in Thomas does not contain an explanation as it does in Mark, the first New Testament Gospel thought to have become published before 70 CE. If that is true, all or parts the Gospel of Thomas were together before or shortly after Jesus died.

Second, the content of the Gospel of Thomas expresses emotionally moving, practical wisdom instead of the abstract, blind belief religious theology that is found in many other early Christian texts. Thus, religious and nonreligious people that are interested in personal development may find the content enlightening.

A third reason for the intense interest in Thomas concerns the first sentence in the Gospel of Thomas in which Jesus is identified as the author, as shown below:

Gospel Prologue

These

are

the words,

Those

hidden,

Which

Jesus,

Who

lives,

Spoke.

Despite the fact that no other early Christian text begins with such a hugely remarkable claim, scholars have generally dismissed the possibility that Jesus composed the Gospel for various reasons:

We possess no historical evidence that Jesus composed a Book before he died. Such a Book should have been well known. However, if what Jesus wrote was so inflammatory, so revolutionary, and such a threat to secular and religious authorities that anyone caught with such a Book might be killed, it would have been hidden for years.

Scholars also point to the fact that the Gospel of Thomas was known by that title, and not as the "Gospel of Jesus," as early as the beginning of the third century.[4] However, that title may not mean anything because most early works were not titled as composed by their original authors. For example, we do not know for sure who authored the Gospels in the New Testament.

It was common in the first few centuries CE for communities to give their works legitimacy by labeling them as having been written by people with close ties to Jesus.[5]

A fourth reason for the massive interest in the Gospel of Thomas concerns the degree to which its content diverges from current Christian theology. In it, we find no trace of Paul's notions that one is "saved" because he believes in:

1. Original sin,

2. That Jesus died on the cross to wipe out Original sin, and

3. That Jesus was resurrected.

Jesus died in 30 CE. Paul composed his first letters in about 50 CE. If Jesus composed all of the material in the Gospel of Thomas, or someone shortly after Jesus collected material and added them to what Jesus composed, we would expect that the Book would not include any references to Paul's theology, which is the case. We have no historical record of Jesus believing in Original Sin or any of Paul's other core ideas.

A fifth reason that the Gospel of Thomas is fascinating to students of early Christianity is that scholars know that the Evangelists, Mark, Luke, Matthew, and John were selecting from one or more larger collections of Jesus' compositions. Much is being written about whether the Gospel of Thomas was one of the early sources of information for the Evangelists.[6]

A sixth reason to study it: Thomas is not a biographical account of Jesus' life; it does not mention his passion and crucifixion, as we would expect that from a Gospel put together after his death. These factors therefore indicate that the Gospel was composed before Jesus died.

Let us remember that the Gospel was discovered 1945. The text is in ancient Coptic, a language understood by few scholars at the time of the discovery. It was not until the 1970's that enough people learned Coptic to translate it and begin studying it.

Therefore, we are in the very early stages of understanding the nature of this magnificent Book.

Semitic Parallelism and the Organization of Thomas

Many do not realize, but almost all of the Books of the Bible were originally composed mentally, memorized, edited mentally, recited to others, and passed down through the generations as an oral work. Eventually, when the Books encountered someone wealthy enough to purchase expensive writing materials and pay a scribe, they were written down. All of this was possible because people had learned a way to organize compositions in their mind for easy recall. This method has been named "Semitic Parallelism."

Semitic Parallelism fell out of fashion among authors after the second century CE. As writing materials became less expensive, and as more people began to use the written word, it became possible for authors to compose quickly at their desks rather than in their heads by following difficult Semitic rules. For those reasons, people lost the ability to recognize, much less use, Semitic Parallelism.

Today, very few people know about the existence of Semitic Parallelism. Through careful study, I have discovered many of the rules that these ancient Semitic authors used to organize their works. When I first applied these insights to the Gospel of Thomas fifteen years ago, it was immediately obvious that many of the contemporary ideas about the Book were wrong. Let me explain:

Because no one has found a coherent organization for the Gospel of Thomas, people do not think that it was composed by a single author. Instead, scholars believe that it is either a collection of sayings or a collection of collections of sayings.

It has been observed that some of the sayings are grouped around what are called "catchwords." For example, the word "kingdom" is found in a group of sayings. They theorize that someone was reminded of sayings by that catchword. That prompted him to put sayings with the word "kingdom" near each other.[7] However, groups of sayings gathered around catchwords do not equal a coherently organized Book with a single main theme and related sub themes. Therefore, again, all scholars think that one person collected the sayings in the Book, or collected a bunch of collections of sayings and combined them into a single volume.

That is what I was expecting when I read Thomas for the first time. However, because I had been intensively studying Semitic Parallelism for over 35 years, I was able to read the Book according to those ancient rules. I therefore recognized that the Gospel did possess its own organization. I concluded that it was not a collective volume, but rather, it was most likely composed by a single person with a single vision which he expressed in a unified Book.

The Gospel of Thomas uses Semitic Parallelism in ingeniously intricate ways; therefore, I concluded initially that the author was either making up his own rules, or that I had an incomplete understanding of the ancient rules. The latter proved to be the case.

After more study, I discovered more rules and was able to determine that the Gospel consists not of *sayings*, but of *poems*. The line, stanza, and parts follow principles no one else has discovered yet. Once I made these discoveries, the meanings of the metaphors became apparent. With that understanding, I could then discern the meaning of each stanza and determine how they each contributed to the meaning of the entire Poem.

The Organization of Books of the Bible

I later applied the complete set of Semitic Parallelism rules to the Garden of Eden Allegory in Genesis, to parts of the Book of Samuel, and to the Gospels of the New Testament. I found that they disclosed the organization, and more importantly, the meanings of those works as they have not been recognized in over 1800 years.

Non students of the Bible may not be shocked by what I have found. However, such a discovery will disrupt not only much of the contemporary Bible scholarship, but also much of the theology that underpins the three Abrahamic religions.

Suggestions

I suggest that everyone begin by understanding the Way of Wisdom in this volume. If you use the website along with the book, you will be able to participate in text discussions, and later in video chat discussions.

After finishing *Volume One*, I suggest that students of the Bible read *Volume Two*, in which I teach Semitic Parallelism. Those not interested in that topic may wish to skip to *Volume Three*.

Endnotes

[1] Elaine Pagels, Beyond Belief, the Secret Gospel of Thomas, (Random House, 1995).

[2] Marvin W. Meyer, James M. Robinson, The Nag Hammadi Scriptures: The Revised and Updated Translation of Sacred Gnostic Texts Complete in One Volume, 2009, Introduction

[3] Robert E. Van Voorst, Jesus Outside the New Testament: an introduction to the ancient evidence, (Grand Rapids: Eerdmans, 2000), pp 187-193.

[4] Meyer, Robinson, Introduction

[5] Paul J. Achtemeier, The Gospel of Mark, The Anchor Bible Dictionary, Double day, p. 545.

[6] James D. Tabor, The Jesus Dynasty, The Hidden History of Jesus, His royal Family and the Birth of Christianity, Simon & Schuster, 2006, 259-71.

[7] Stephen J. Patterson, The Gospel of Thomas and Jesus, Polebridge Press, 1993.

CHAPTER TWO

JESUS' GOSPEL: BECOME FULLY HUMAN

How a person views human nature determines how they think about the causes of conflict within themselves and between individuals and groups. Those on Jesus' Way, here called the "Way of Wisdom," view human nature in a manner opposite to those following what I call the "Way of Religion." Therefore, they resolve conflict in a strikingly different manner.

THE TWO MEANS OF KNOWING

We encounter the following poem six times in the Gospel of Thomas:

> He
>
> Who
> has his ear (sg.)[1]
> to listen,[2]
>
> Let him
> listen.[3]

[1] *Ear*: Third-ear.

[2] *Listen*: Soul-listen.

[3] *Listen*: Soul-listen.

I will later present evidence that the Gospel also ended with this poem.

Ways of Wisdom and Religion

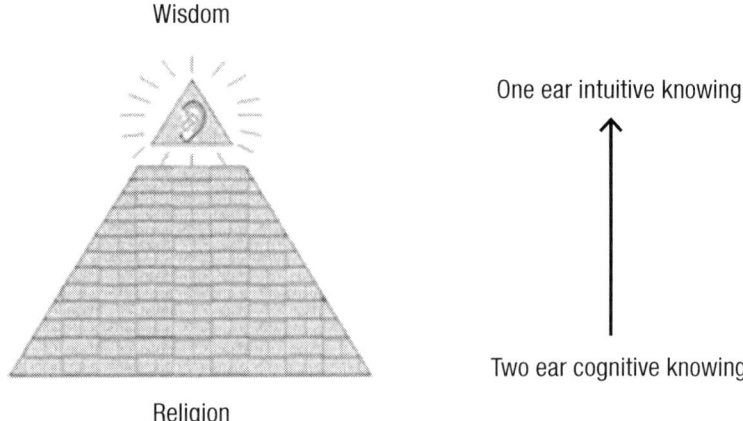

BECOME A KINGDOM

According to Jesus, when one uses self-directed intuition properly, he enters a type of kingdom where he rules wisely over himself and his interactions with others. He defines this kingdom in Chapter Two, Poem Two (Saying Three) as follows:

The kingdom,	[1] *Eye*: Third-eye
It is of your eye[1] inward,[2]	[2] *It is of your eye inward*: It is a means of looking inward at yourself with your third-eye.
And it is of your eye outward.[3]	[3] *It is of your eye outward*: It is a means of looking outward at others and the world with your third-eye.

"The kingdom…" A person as a kingdom.

Jesus tells us that when we evolve, we become what he calls a kingdom, or a field of regal influence. Think of the core self within each of us as projecting a radiation field. It affects every cell in our body and it emanates out to affect others.

For example, we all know that when we are fully alive and full of joy, one with our personal power, our bodies feel different, and when we walk into a room, everyone seems to notice. When we are like that, we know we have become more a king or queen over our kingdom, that is, our field of influence.

"It is of your eye inward…" The kingdom is an evolved means of knowing oneself with one's third, intuitive eye.

Above, Jesus points to our third ear as a source of intuitive knowing. Now, he tells us that we have also a third eye. Both enable us to "soul-know," the term I will use for third ear and third-eye knowing.

"It is of your eye outward." The kingdom is an intuitive third eye means of knowing others and the world.

As a person evolves on Jesus' Way of Wisdom, he increasingly rules over himself and his interactions with others. He, thus, becomes more a king or queen, a fully developed, independent, self-joyful person. The contrast is a person who has not evolved to rule over himself or his interactions with others. Instead, his social conditioning and the expectations of others rules him.

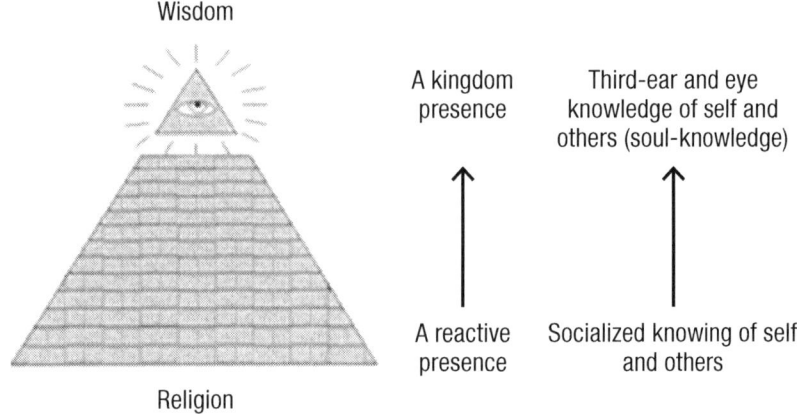

THE SOUL-KNOWING PROCESS

We all instinctively know that what we perceive through our physical senses does not tell the entire story. Therefore, many people, especially creative types, seek a means to break out of their routine, indoctrinated means of perceiving, in order to discover the reality that is hidden from them.

My friend Tom, an artist, recently sent me an email in which he described his soul knowing creative process. I quote it below because it details the process that many use to see reality:

> "When I become totally engaged in painting, I sometimes arrive at a place of calm, a place where I don't think about the strength of my composition or what color to choose, because that all happens automatically and I experience (though I don't know this until later) the stillness that comes as a result of "turning off" the left side of my brain and the associated ego with all its noisy worries and fears, dreams and resentments, sorrows, joys and puzzle solving. In that ego-less state, in the stillness I refer to as 'getting out of my own way,' my right brain takes in the images and other information that I need."

Tom described his process of excavating information that is hidden from him. That information is the image that he puts on canvas. His process has five stages:

First, he becomes "ego-less." He has told me that when he paints to make money or to gain a reputation, he cannot soul-see.

Second, he becomes willing to abandon his prevailing ideas and expectations for the work.

Third, he achieves stillness. He has certain places and rituals that enable him to find quietude. He knows that when his mind is in a state of regret, worry, or excitement, he cannot soul-know. These mental states hinder his ability to be present in the moment.

Fourth, he allows information to come to him freely and flow through him without judging it. He lets the force of his intuition move his hand.

Fifth, he inspects what he senses and decides what to do with it through left-brain analysis. However, his left-brain never takes over the process, always working with his right-brain. In other words, he tempers the right-brain's creativity with the left-brain's rationality. He discovers the meaning of what his right-brain provides with the left side of his brain.

Notice, that during the entire process, he uses his right-brain to receive information and his left to shape it. When we do the reverse, we turn off our soul-knowing.

Ways of Wisdom and Religion

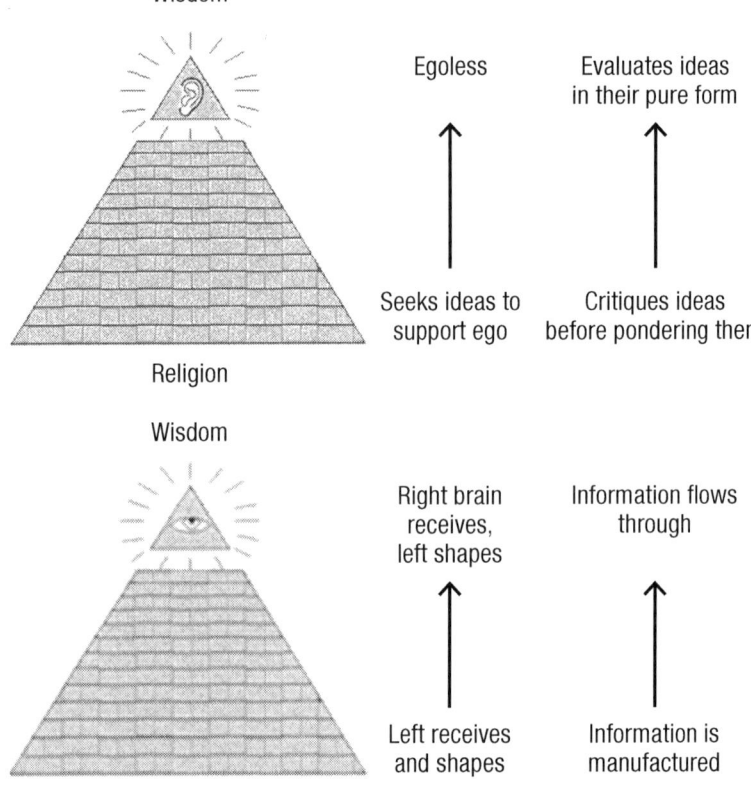

Jesus describes the soul-knowing process in Poem Two from Chapter Eight, Saying 27):

If *you* *do* *not make the Sabbath* *outward*[1]	[1]*Sabbath outward*: A normal Sabbath Day when one does not work. Metaphorically, one rests in stillness.
The Sabbath *inward*[2]	[2]*Sabbath inward*: A time of internal stillness. A time of living in the present rather than the past or future.
	[3]*Peer*: Soul-seeing.
You *will peer*[3] *not* *upon the Father.*[4,5]	[4]*Father*: Jesus calls the male aspect of God, "Father." (He will later talk about his God "Mother").
	[5]*Peer not upon the Father*: Jesus maintains that if we use soul-knowing deeply, we can experience the divine in everyone and everything.

"If you do not make the Sabbath outward, the Sabbath inward," If you do not actualize the external ritual of rest by being still within yourself...

Jesus expressed that one cannot soul-know unless he is present in the here and now. When we are internally distracted by the past and future, we are perceiving through our physical senses (two eyes, two ears); that is, we are socially-knowing, letting society's beliefs shape our perceptions.

"You will peer not..." You will not soul-see.

"You will peer not upon the Father." You will not soul-see the Father. In other words, you will not *experience* the Father. Instead, you will either blindly believe or disbelieve in Him.

That Poem, thus, expresses Jesus' understanding that one need *not believe* in God, because through soul-knowing, it is possible to *experience* God.

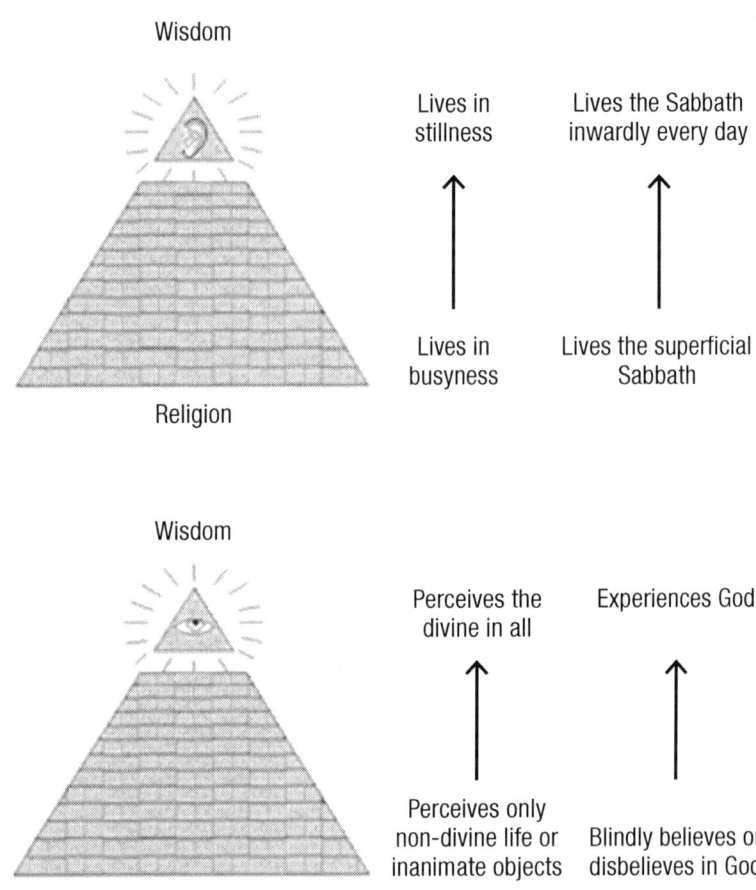

Jazz guitarist Larry Carlton described soul-knowing like this:

> "When I was in College, 19 years old, there was an upright bass player, student, keyboard player, and myself, and a sax player—we were all about the same age, and we were all very passionate about jazz. We got together one Friday night in someone's front room to jam. That evening was the first for me because I experienced for the first time going to the "zone" musically. Before that I had always played...and played a lot 6 nights a week in clubs, and so I had been playing 13 to 14 years by then. However, that night we played (he strums a chord). I went to the zone during my solo...which means...I don't want to make this to sound cliché, but I became one with the instrument that night. What I knew how to play, and what I had been playing was transcended that night to another level to where for the first time I became not in control of the guitar, but one with the guitar. What happened is...I played chorus after chorus after chorus, it is like experiencing runners high if you are a runner, where you do not need any effort any more, you are just running, you don't feel anything...well, that happened that night. And I just played chorus after chorus after chorus. I was loving the experience. Pretty soon the bass dropped out, and now it was just me and the piano player, and pretty soon the piano player stopped playing. But my awareness was so in touch with this that I just kept playing. And I don't know if I played two more choruses or five more choruses, I don't remember the details of it, but I remember coming out of it, and opening my eyes and they were all just sitting there looking at me, because they had experienced it with me. That was the first time that my maturity level as a musician went to that place of connecting

> *with my instrument. That experience...once you experience it, you want to experience it again. So, my life's goal is to try to go to that place when I am playing the guitar. I pick up the instrument in a setting that has the potential, whether it's with the blues band or jamming with a guy, my whole objective is to get to that place where I am connecting with my instrument and feel that experience again."*

Larry becomes one with his instrument when he soul-knows. Those around him could tell that he was different and they loved what was coming *through* him. That is the type of knowing that Jesus emphasizes as the foundation to his Way of Wisdom.

Tom puts his discoveries on canvas for others to see; Larry puts his into music; Jesus put his in poems for others to see and reflect on.

All of us soul-know to be creative. All of us seek to be one with all. This is what we seek through drugs, thrills, romance, and candlelit dinners. Few of us develop the discipline and courage to soul-know like wise people do.

Throughout time, people desiring personal growth have found it necessary to retreat from their daily routines to obtain hidden information by soul-knowing. Some Native American tribes encourage their members to use the sweat lodge to soul-sense visions to improve their lives. Spiritual people all over the world attend retreats led by trained spiritual guides who assist people in "listening." All of them are discovering the meaning of hidden information.

Many cultures revere those who specialize in soul-knowing, calling them "seers," "mystics," "shamans," and "prophets." Literature and oral traditions from these cultures describe the conditions for hearing hidden words. One generally must:

- Go apart, that is, get away from the influence of the ideas of others,

- Become still,

- Abandon expectations and prevailing beliefs,

- Be open to new ideas,

- Be willing to see visions, hear words, and sense vague impressions,

- Trust what one hears and sees,

- Ponder what has been heard and seen,

- Discern how to use the new information in one's life,

- Formulate new tentative beliefs about how to be a more evolved person, and

- Have the fortitude to live differently in the face of opposition.

Jesus did those things to reveal to himself how to live a more fulfilled life. He then structured his insights into the poems that we find in this Gospel.

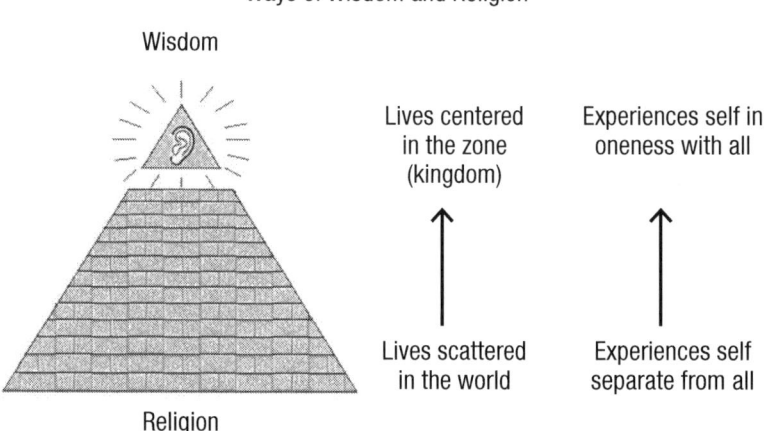

Jesus composed every Poem in the Gospel by revealing his "hidden" wisdom with soul-knowing. That is stated in the Prologue, Poem One in Chapter One (Saying 1a):

These
are
the words,[1]

Those
hidden,[2]

Which
Jesus,[3]

Who
lives,[4]

Spoke[5]

[1] *These are the words*: These are the words of wisdom that make up this Book.

[2] *Those hidden*: Those hidden by our socialization.

[3] *Which Jesus*: (Implied) Which Jesus soul-discovered and applied to his life.

[4] *Who lives*: Who lives fully as an evolved, fulfilled human being.

[5] *Spoke*: He spoke out to the world to enlighten others.

In Part Three of the first Poem in the Book, he tells us his purpose:

Whoever[1]
discovers the meaning
of these words,[2]

Will take a taste
not
of death.[3]

[1] *Whoever*: Whoever soul-listens.

[2] *Whoever discovers the meaning of these words*: Whoever discovers the meaning of these words for their own lives.

[3] *Will take a taste not of death*: Will not be living death.

"Whoever discovers the meaning of these words." Whoever uses my insights as a stimulus to discover their own answers.

"Will not take a taste of death." Will be led by their soul-knowing out of slavery to society and its endless doctrines to living a fulfilled life of one's own.

Jesus unearthed the wisdom that was hidden behind his socialized blindness, discovered its meaning, and become fully alive. Jesus saw that wisdom surrounds us, is in us, and is us. He experienced that wisdom as a person; and addressed him as his "Father." He thus tells us that our "Father" gives us access to the answers we need. We are not individuals wandering in the world alone. Implied in every poem are his core discoveries:

1. Everyone receives unique information tailored to bring him to fulfillment.

2. All of that information comes wrapped in love.

3. All of that information is hidden by our prevailing belief systems.

4. Nothing happens by accident. It is all designed to lead us to fulfillment.

5. All of our "death" emotions arise because we do not understand this design.

His conclusions are verified when we cease social-knowing and begin using our soul-knowing.

For example, if we were taught to believe that democracy is good and socialism is bad, we will see democracy as our salvation and socialism as our ruin. We will look for evidence to support our preconceptions. Further, we will distort evidence to confirm these preconceptions. We may even sacrifice and die for our indoctrinated beliefs.

That is the Way of Religion. When we follow that path, we base our lives on other people's ideas. We become so blind and deaf that we do not know that we are blind and deaf. This is not freedom, it is slavery.

We all impose patterns on reality in order to understand it. For example, some people are skeptics, some see evil around every corner, some are positive-thinkers, and some are atheists. Jesus presents us with alternate patterns for our consideration. As we choose our perceptual patterns, we choose our lives. With soul-knowing we can examine the evidence in support of our tentative beliefs.

Jesus poetically presents alternate ways of viewing our situations. He also empowers us to verify his observations for ourselves. Thus, he facilitates rather than indoctrinates.

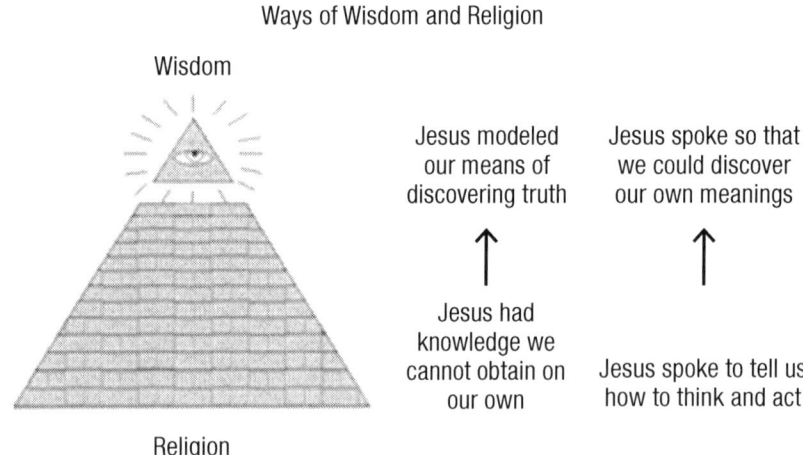

Ways of Wisdom and Religion

Ways of Wisdom and Religion

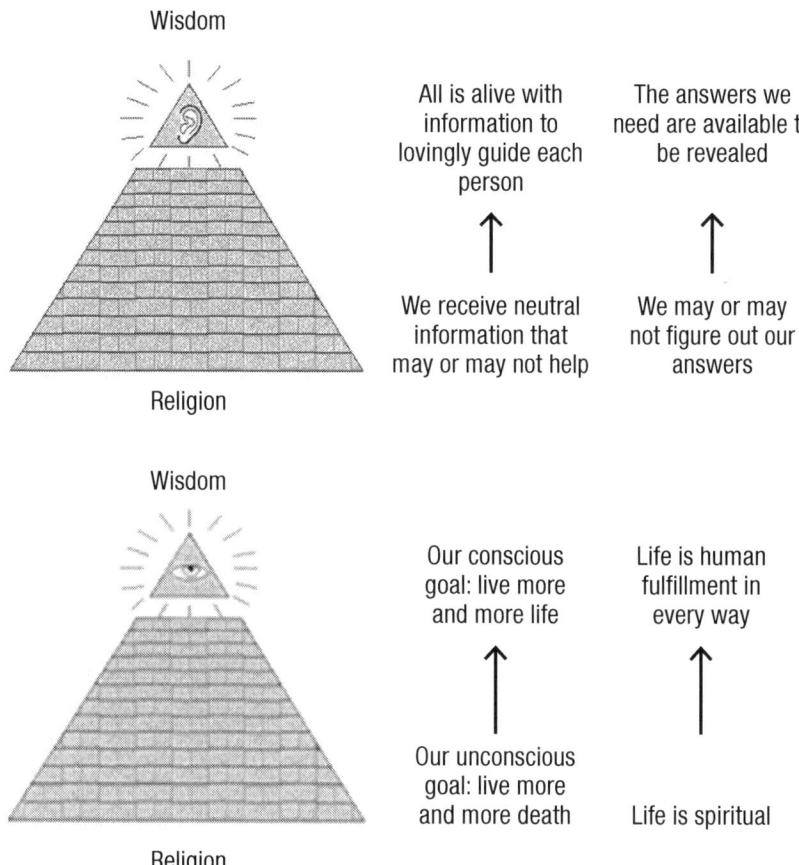

THE WORLD

The "world" for Jesus is people who primarily use what I call, "socialized knowing." Instead of using their intuitive soul-knowing to know themselves and others most or all of the time, their knowledge of themselves and others arises primarily from what they have been taught by others. To facilitate people to be on his Way of Wisdom, Jesus taught them to leave the world and enter a community of kingdom people. He says that in Poem Two from Chapter Eight, (Saying 27):

Jesus said this:

If you do not fast from the world, [1,2]

You will discover not the kingdom. [3]

[1] *World*: People who primarily use their two eyes and ears to know themselves, others, and the nature of the universe. People who socially-know rather than soul-know.

[2] *If you do not fast from the world*: If you do not starve yourself from soul-knowers. If you do not leave your Ways of Religion.

[3] *You will discover not the kingdom.* You will not discover yourself as an independent, insightful knower of yourself, others, and the principles governing human growth and interaction.

"If you do not fast from the world…" If you do not leave the influence of your parents, teachers, clergy, peers, media, and other authorities who have taught us how to think and act…

As I pointed out in the Introduction, when a person identifies with a set of theological or secular beliefs, he creates a *Way of Religion*. Those beliefs were not native to him as a newborn child. The "world" taught them to him.

When we identify with a religion, that is, *a set of beliefs held by others*, we defend and promote that religion as we do ourselves. Unconsciously, our religions become an extension of ourselves. We also promote and defend our indoctrinators (parents, teachers, clergy, politicians, media-idols, peers, etc.) because they are representatives of our world.

"If you do not fast from the world..." Jesus says strongly: If you do not leave your socialized world, all your Ways of Religion, you will not follow me, you will not find yourself, you will not be a kingdom, and you will not be fulfilled.

"You will discover not the kingdom." You will not discover on your own how to rule over yourself and your interactions with others. Instead, you will forever be a mental slave to society and its multitude of theological and secular religions.

In short, fast from the world and you may discover yourself and become a free and independent person; or do not fast from the world and you will become an evermore naïve, reactive serf. Self-rule is fundamental to rejection of the world.

We don't "discover" by listening to sermons, political speeches or school lectures, which I will call "social-knowing." We don't rule by placing the authority of indoctrinators and their doctrines above the authority that we personally hold over ourselves.

The kingdom is a state of being independent from the beliefs of others. To discover it, one must question and suspend all that he has learned through his physical eyes and ears in order to attain soul-knowing of reality through his faculty of intuition.

Ways of Wisdom and Religion

Ways of Wisdom and Religion

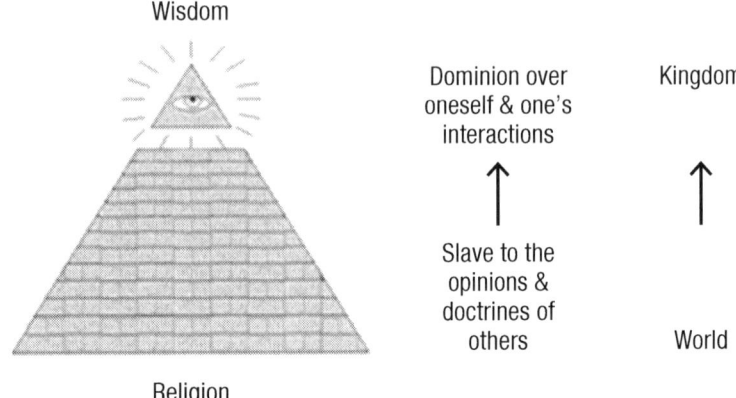

Discover Rather than Believe

We all have lenses through which we view the world. They consist of the beliefs we bring with us to our acts of physical sensing. Instead of observing reality, our preexisting beliefs compel us to see and hear what we want to see and hear.

With respect to seeing, as we peel away the first layer of belief lenses, we understand more. The more we peel off layers, the more we will get closer and closer to the truth.

Jesus states his core principle for becoming a kingdom in many poems. Here is another from Chapter 21, Poem 4 (Saying 110):

Jesus said this:

Whoever has discovered the world,[1]

And he comes to be rich,[2]

Let him abdicate from the world.[3]

[1] *Whoever has discovered the world*: Whoever has used his soul-knowing to discover his enslavement to the Ways of Religion.

[2] *And he comes to be rich*: And he becomes a self-confident ruler of himself and his interactions based on his adopted beliefs.

[3] *Let him abdicate from the world*: Let him give up that rule to discover himself on his own.

"Whoever has discovered the world..." Whoever has removed his belief filters to see the true nature of the world...

Our belief filters are not easily removed, because our present false reality is a part of our identity. Thus, to know more truly, we must die to the oneself and be born again in enlightenment.

Our belief filters are also difficult to remove because we are rewarded by our peers for conforming to their ways of thinking and acting, because that makes them comfortable. People generally do not trust or enjoy the presence of those who disrupt the status quo. However, clearly, Jesus only sought out and encouraged rebels.

Courage is a necessary quality of those who follow the Way of Wisdom. It is a continual process of painfully destroying cherished beliefs, thereby creating a new awareness and self.

"And he comes to be rich..." And he comes to be a ruler of himself and others based on his firm, adopted beliefs

Those following the Way of Religion believe that their Way is the absolute truth. They use that knowledge to feel self-confident, that is, to rule themselves and their interactions. Those following the Way of Wisdom live their lives in constant pursuit of the truth. Those following the Way of Religion live arrogantly and stagnate in their blind faith. Those following the Way of Wisdom die to themselves and their faith to be reborn in their true natures, continually discovering themselves, others, God and the nature of the world.

"Let him abdicate from the world..." Let him permit others to follow the fools' means of obtaining self-confidence.

Jesus did not indoctrinate people with beliefs that they could proudly use to rule themselves and others. Instead, he led people off the Way of Religion and onto the Way of Wisdom. His kingdom is a Way of independently standing alone against the belief-rulers of the world, together with others following the same Way.

Therefore, the kingdom is a non-doctrine-based way of living for the individual and groups. It incorporates everyone who dedicates themselves to leaving their secular and theological religions in favor of the path of perpetual discovery.

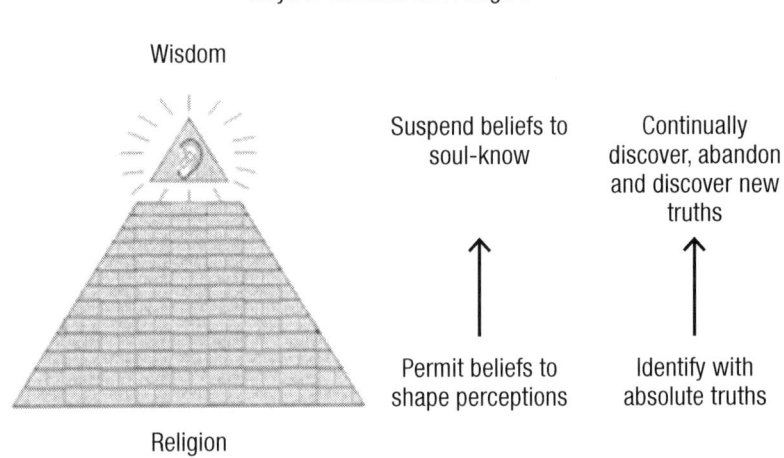

BECOME LIKE A LITTLE CHILD

Jesus and others following the Way of Wisdom view a newborn differently than those on the Way of Religion. We see that in Chapter Two, Poem Three (Saying 4) of the Gospel of Thomas.

Jesus said this:

*He
will delay
not,*[1]

*Namely
the man
of maturity
in his days,*[2,3]

[1] *He will delay not*: He will immediately.

[2] *He of maturity*: Especially the one who has become conscious and alive at a high level of wisdom.

[3] *Days*: Times of enlightenment. As opposed to nights, which are times of intellectual slavery.

To ask a little,
small child,

He
being
of seven days,[5]

About the place[6]
of life;[7]

And[8]
he
will live.[9]

For
there
are
many first,[10]

Who
will come to be
last;[11]

And
they
will come to be
single ones.[12]

[5]*Seven*: The child is born complete; he has not been corrupted by the world.

[6]*Place*: That place within, from which we think and act.

[7]Life: A fulfilled way of living.

[8]*And*: And learning from a small child…

[9]*He will live*: He will be fulfilled by modeling the child.

[10]*There are many first*: There are many wise people.

[11]*Who will come to be last*: Who will seek to learn from those others regarded as "last," such a little, small child.

[12]*Single one*: Congruent ones. A little, small child is congruent with their true natures.

"He will delay not, namely the man of maturity in his days to ask a little, small child, he being of seven days, about the place of life." A wise man will not make anything more important than seeking to be more alive. He looks for a model for his life, not in his theological beliefs, in adults, in books, but in a newborn.

Most people do not seek "life" as their first priority when they get up in the morning. A wise person does.

To grow, most people talk to therapists, their clergy, their friends, read books, or reflect. A wise person gets out of his head, away from adults, and observes life in its purest form.

Jesus was an acute observer. He did not use abstract logical speculation or deduction, primarily. He was a poet, not a theologian. He was a phenomenological therapist and philosopher, not a behavioral psychologist or objective philosopher. He ignored his mental musings and delved into his experience to understand how he might evolve. He was primarily seeking a model, not an idea.

Ways of Wisdom and Religion

Wisdom

Seeks a tactile model of life

↑

Seeks abstract spiritual life

Religion

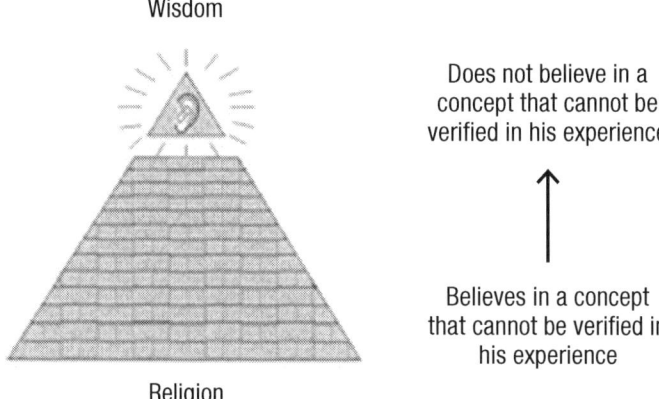

Ways of Wisdom and Religion

"Ask a little, small child, he being of seven days," Ask an overlooked little child, or an adult who is like a little child.

We sometimes live in confusion because we cannot discern the difference between people living fully alive from those living less alive. That results in us not possessing real life goals for ourselves. Instead, we wander around, adoring this false life in one person, and that one in another. We dress ourselves in this way of being, and then in that one—never finding our true selves.

Sometimes we encounter a very alive person, and instead of humbly modeling them, we either become embarrassed that we are not that alive, or become jealous of their life. The wise seek out those more alive, study them and humble themselves to learn from them.

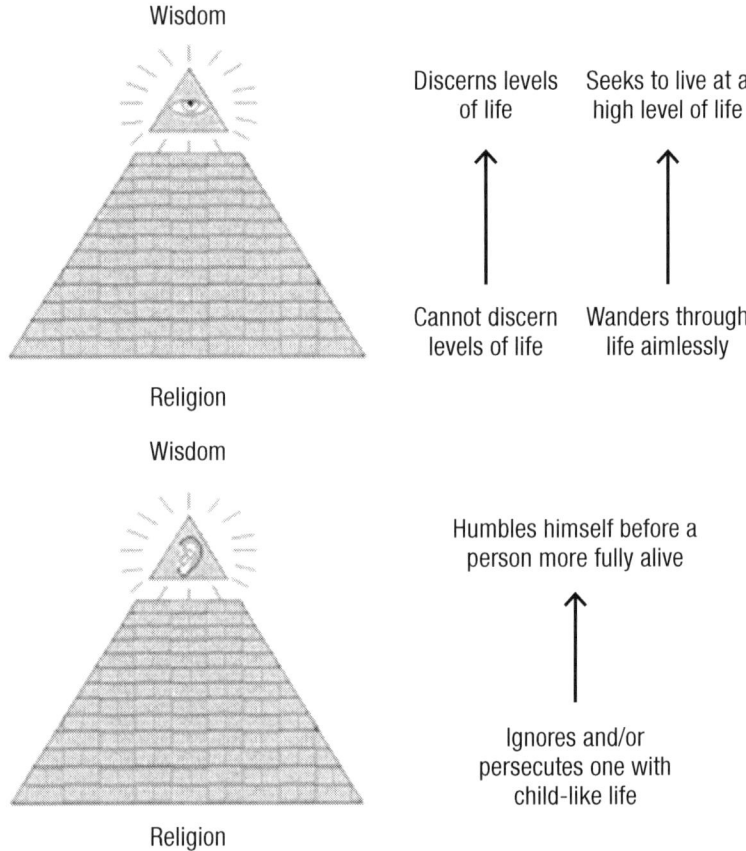

"Ask a little, small child, he being of seven days, about the place of life." Observe beyond appearances at the source of life in a new born.

Some look at a little child and see original sin as the source of his life. Others may not even look for the source. A wise person becomes fascinated at the "place" within a little child from which he lives.

"To ask" is the first step in the wisdom-seeking process. If we do not recognize the lack of life in ourselves, we will not ask one to show it to us. If we do not humble ourselves to ask, we do not evolve.

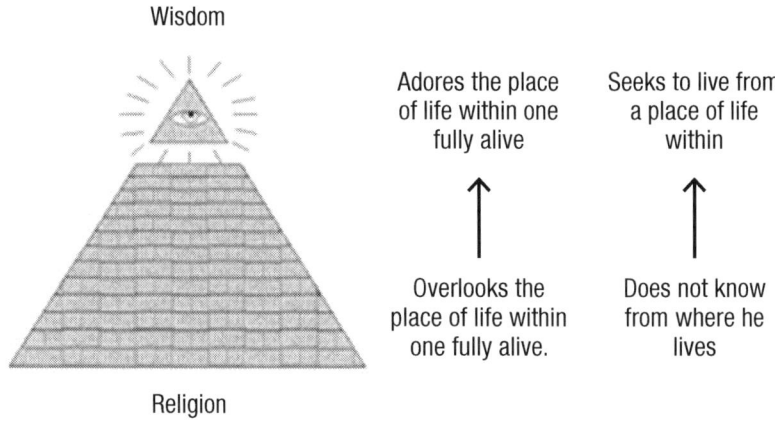

"And they will come to be single ones:" And they will come to be congruent with their core selves.

Most of us, if not all of us, are to some extent divided between our true and false selves. We can illustrate that like this:

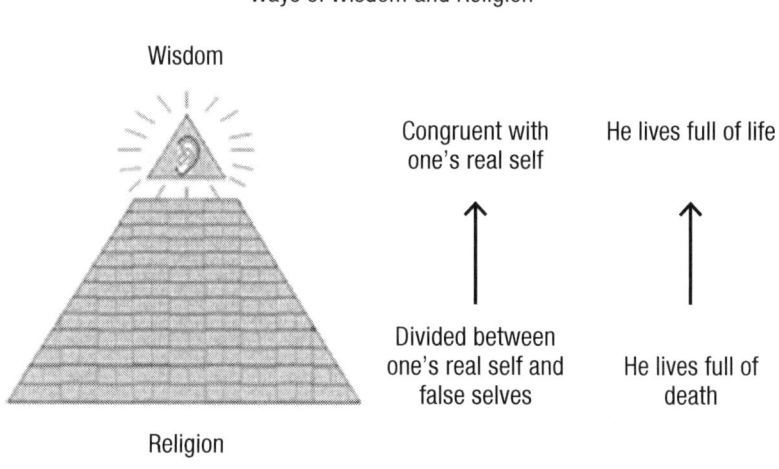

Jesus does not distinguish between a spiritual life and a personal life. They are the same. When we develop ourselves, we develop our whole selves. His formula for personal development is this: Abandon your false selves and live congruent with your true self. You will then be more evolved spiritually, mentally, and emotionally.

When we identify with a false self, we identify with a set of beliefs. For example, if one identifies with being a Christian, he chooses to *be* not himself primarily, but the doctrine of some church. That doctrine becomes part of his false self. He will promote and defend it as if it were his real self.

In another example, if one labels himself a "conservative," he tells himself and the world that he believes certain things. In other words, he has established an artificial identity.

If one chooses to identify with his possessions, he identifies with the beliefs associated with his things and money, not with his true self.

The little child does not crawl around believing this and that. He does not say, "I am smart, I am black, I am Asian, I am an American, I am a Muslim, I am rich," or "I am poor." He does not invest himself in beliefs about those false identities. He just is—and he is fulfilled in life. That is why he is Jesus' model of wisdom.

Through socialization, we learn to think and behave in particular ways. We invest ourselves in our false selves enough to promote and defend them as if they were our true selves. They are not. We have created them from our own amalgamation of socially accepted beliefs. Thus, we become divided from who we are, resulting in a kind of living death.

Ways of Wisdom and Religion

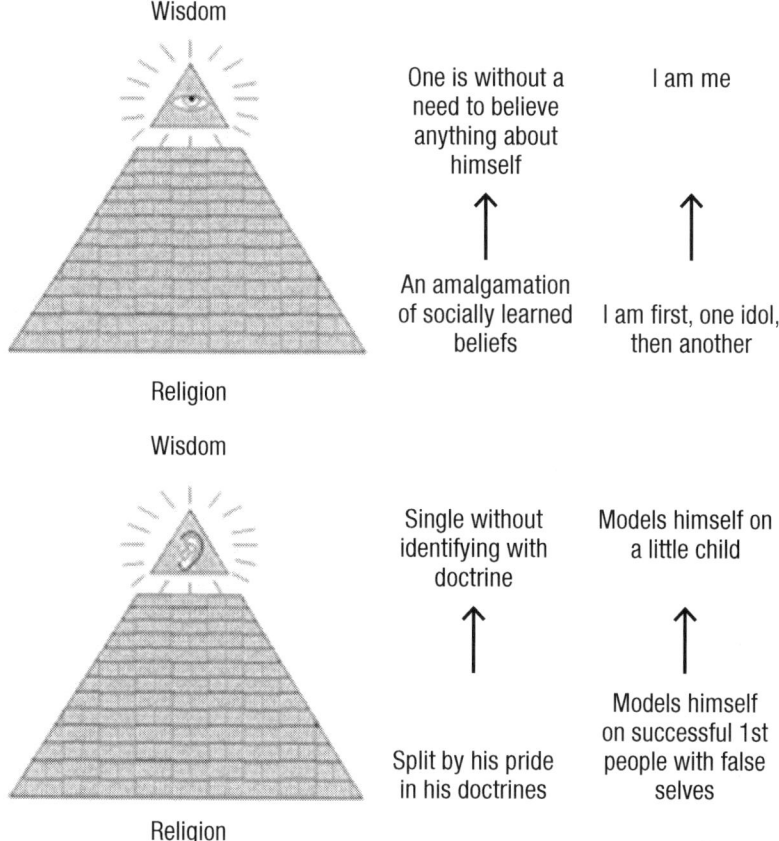

"For there are many first, who will come to be last." For there are many who think that they are first because they identify with a superior-to-others false self, who then become humble by recognizing that in fact, they are last to one full of life. Then, because they seek to evolve, they become "last" when they "ask" one modeling life to teach them about their "place" of life.

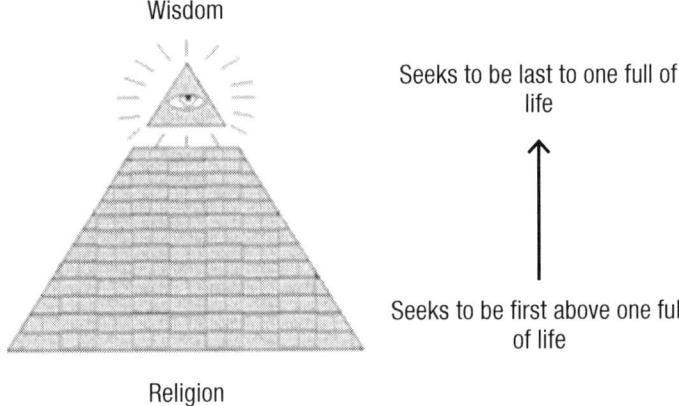

DISTINGUISH BETWEEN LIGHT AND DARKNESS IN PEOPLE

According to Jesus, we enter the world living light. In Chapter 13, Poem Two (Saying 61) he explains how we live darkness.

When he should come to be divided,[1]	[1] *When he should come to be divided*: When he should come to be divided between his true self and his many false selves.
He will be full of darkness.[2]	[2] *He will be full of darkness*: He will be opaque and dishonest.

"When he should come to be divided," When we should come to be divided between our true and false selves.

"He will be full of darkness." He will be full of dishonesty.

Jesus does not use the word "evil" or "sin" in this *Gospel*. Instead, he says that we become "dark when we divide from the true self that we are at birth. When we do that, we lie, because we proclaim ourselves to be what we are not.

Consequently, Jesus' formulated the two laws of the Way of Wisdom that we find in Chapter Two, Poem Six (Saying 6b):

Jesus responded: "You do not speak lies,[1] And what you hate in him,[2] You do not do to him."[3]	[1] *You do not speak lies:* You do not live through a false self. You do not live through any religious or secular doctrine. [2] *And what you hate in him:* And the false selves that you hate in him. And the incongruence that you hate in him. And the lies that you hate in him. And the Ways of Religion that you hate in him. [3] *You do not do to him:* You do not become what you are not to punish someone who is not what he is.

"Do not lie." Do not be a false self.

In other words, Jesus recognizes that behind all harmful thoughts and actions are lies about what we truly are. When we identify with our religious theology, with our secular doctrine, with the things and people important to us, we lie. Further, when we lie, we become dark. When we become dark, we know it; we suffer and the world suffers.

"And what you hate in him, you do not do to him." And the lie that you hate in him, do not do.

For example, if we hate a politician for not being what he is, we lie and become his twin. To hate a liar is to lie. (Later we will learn how to act toward others who lie).

Ways of Wisdom and Religion

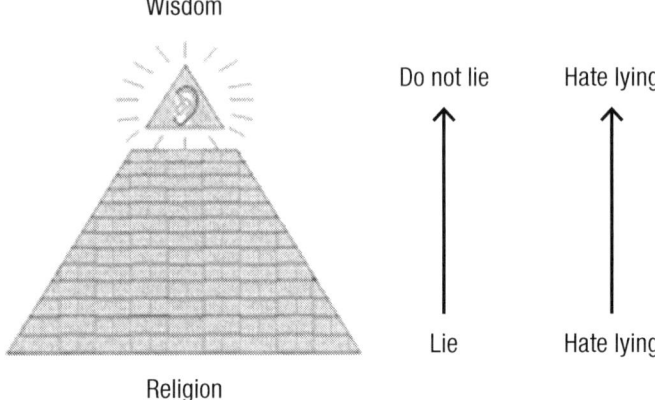

Thus, Jesus counsels us to distinguish two polarities in ourselves: lying and being congruent; and darkness from light. He speaks of being light in Poem Three in Chapter Seven (Saying 24):

He
said to them:

The light[1]
exists inward
of a man
of light,[2,3]

And
he
comes to be
light
to the world,[4,5]

All
of it.[6]

[1] *Light*: The life force that illuminates.

[2] *Man of light*: An adult who has become again congruent with his core self.

[3] *The light exists inward of a man of light*: Divine light is in each of us to the degree that we are light.

[4] *World*: Dishonest people who are divided between their false selves and their real selves. People who lie.

[5] *He comes to be light to the world*: He comes to save the world. He comes to reveal the true nature of dishonesty in the world.

[6] *All of it*: All of the world.

"The light exists inward of a man of light." Divine illuminating power exists in a person to the degree that he chooses to be his core self. When he chooses to be a lie, that is, to identify with his false selves rather than be what he was at birth, he creates darkness within.

Jesus never speaks in this Gospel about an evil Satan outside of ourselves. Rather, he holds us responsible for being light or darkness for ourselves and for the world. In other words, we create ourselves as Satans as we choose to lie.

Ways of Wisdom and Religion

Wisdom

Honestly himself — Divine light in the world

↑ ↑

Dishonestly projects his false selves as his real self — Evil darkness in the world

Religion

When people asked Jesus about the source of light in a child, he responded as follows in Chapter 11, Poem Five (Saying 50) (Remember he reports what he observes, not his logical deductions):

Jesus said this:

If

they[1]

should ask you this:

"You

have

come into being

from where?"[2]

[1] *They*: People who are divided and full of darkness. People on the Way of Religion. People who lie.

[2] *You have come into being from where?* You are not like other people. How did you come to be like that?

Speak to them
this:

"We
have come outward
of the light, ³,⁴

The place⁵

Where
the light
comes to be
there,

Outward
by its own hand;⁶

It
stood itself
on its own feet⁷

And
it
appeared outward
in our appearances."⁸

If
they
should ask you
this:

"Are
you
it?"⁹

³*light:* The divine intelligence and spirit within us.

⁴We have *come outward of the light:* Outward of God. We live from the One who is light, honesty, and congruence.

⁵*Place:* The location within us from which we think and act.

⁶*The light comes to be there outward by its own hand:* "By its own hand" means "by its own control." light is alive. It emanates from us with its own intelligence as it chooses.

⁷*Stood itself on its own feet:* To "stand" is to find one's confidence. To "stand on one's own feet" is find one's confidence in who one is.

⁸*Appearances:* Our unique manifestations of the light. The light-Life is the same in each of us; however, it manifests itself in each person's unique appearance.

⁹*Are you It:* Are you divine light?

Say this:

"We
are
its sons, [10]

And
we
are
the chosen
of the Father[11]

Who
lives."[12]

If
they
should ask you
this:

"What
is
the sign
of your Father[13]

Which
is
in you?"

Say to them
this:

"It
is
movement,

And
it
is
stillness.[14]

[10] *We are its sons*: We possess the same light-life as the light. Yes, we are sons of God.

[11] *Chosen of the Father*: Jesus experienced the Father as choosing to make light manifest in people. The light acts, the Father chooses when and to whom it is to act on.

[12] *Who lives*: Who lives life, as opposed to death and darkness.

[13] *What is the sign of your Father*: What is the observable proof that you are divine?

[14] *It is movement and it is stillness*: It is thought and action from stillness. One can think and act from stillness or from busyness. Movement from stillness is the visible sign of God. We can sense it in ourselves and see it in others who are of the light. Those full of light do not live in the past or the future; they live in the now, in the present.

"We have come outward of the light." We have come outward of God who lives in congruence with his divine life.

We now know more fully what Jesus meant in the previous Poem: **"And he comes to be light to the world, all of it."** He comes to be God to the world, all of God, not a bit of God. Jesus observed that the light is not reduced in a person. He saw the divinity in a little child and in those who are like little children, while others observe original sin or mere personhood.

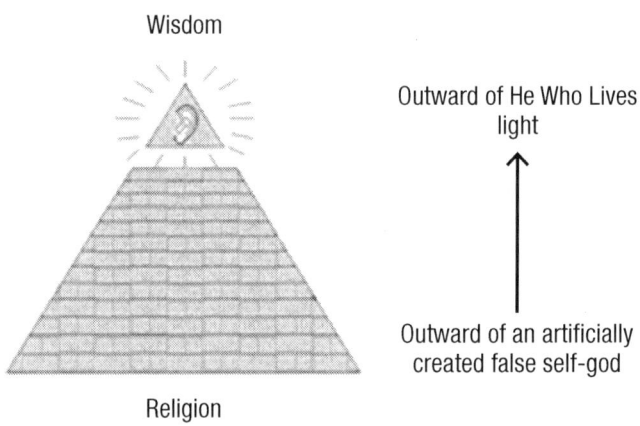

"The light comes to be there outward by its own hand." The light moves as a living force with its own intelligence. It automatically leads people to be congruent with their core selves. It fights them through its absence when they are not.

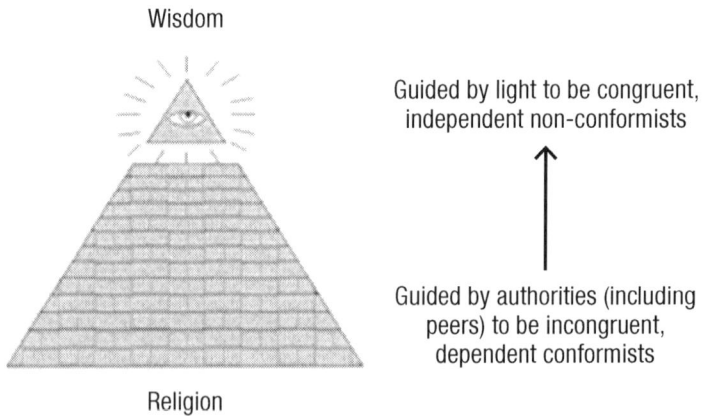

"We are the chosen of the Father." We do not choose light, rather, the light, which is the life of the Father, chooses us. It acts in response to our choice to be light.

The nature of life and light includes two choices, ours and the Father's. Each instant we choose to be congruent or incongruent, to be honest or to be liars, to evolve or to devolve. The light within us responds with more light or its lack, darkness.

Jesus calls the source of light, his "Father." Again, he did not arrive at that conclusion through logical deduction. When he soul-knew a little child, he discovered the Father as the source of the light.

Ways of Wisdom and Religion

"It stood itself on its own feet." The light within us possesses its own dignity. It is what it is and knows itself. A person who possesses it is who he is, and knows himself. He does not need outside approval or justification for any thought or action. He stands, challenging the world, on his own two feet, fortified by the light.

When we live through our false selves, we seek self-confidence by standing, not on our own light, but on our religions. For example, an American stands on his nationhood and its traditions, values, beliefs, rituals and laws; that is, on the doctrine of Americanism. A Muslim stands on his Islamic community and beliefs. A liberal stands on his political faith. A rich man and a poor man stand on their class associations and beliefs.

When we believe that we are something or someone outside ourselves, we stand on sand, a poor foundation. When we stand only on our inner light, our foundations are strong.

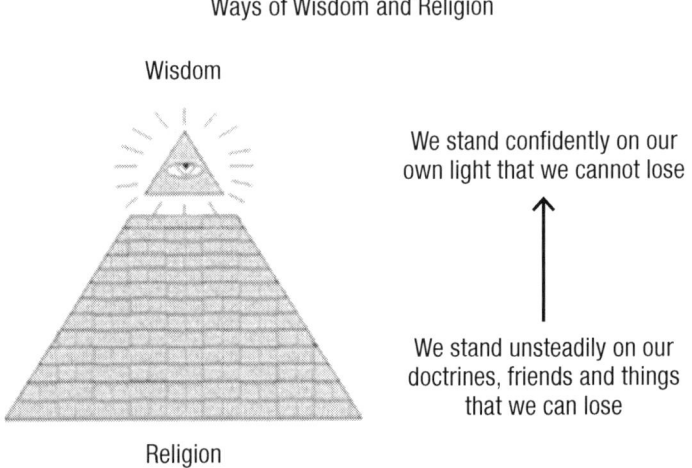

"And it appeared outward in our appearances." The light becomes observable by others in our unique manifestation in the world. Jesus observed that everyone possesses divine light at their core.

People who are happy when others live through their false selves are darkness valuing darkness. When people look through a person's darkness to their light core, they are light penetrating darkness to value the other person's true self.

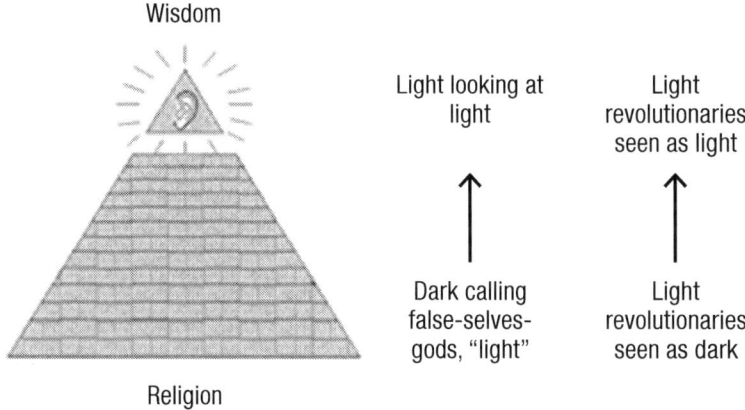

Ways of Wisdom and Religion

"We are its sons." We are all sons and daughters of God.

Jesus does not say that he is *not* the son of God; rather, that we all are. However, we are unevolved sons and daughters. We choose the degree to which we live that divine life and possess the inner light.

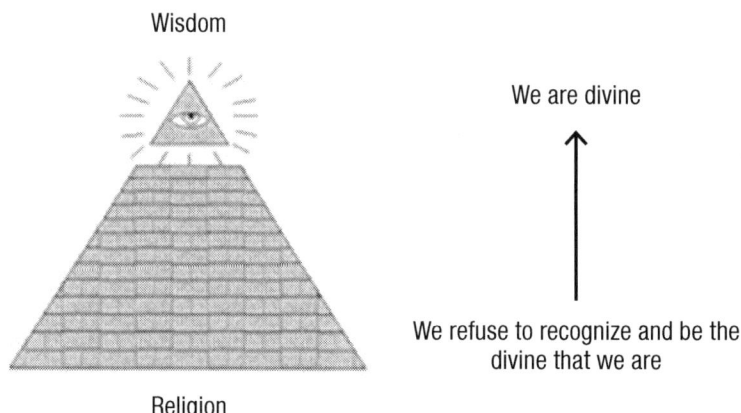

Ways of Wisdom and Religion

"What is the sign of your Father?" What is the tactile proof that you are the son or daughter of God?

How many people go around looking for a sign that God is in a person? Would they even know what to look for?

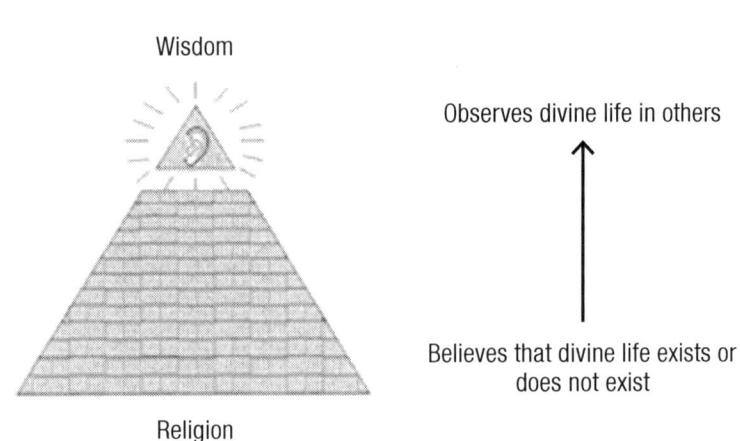

"It is movement and it is stillness." It is a contradiction: movement and stillness at the same time. That is an experience like no other.

When one chooses to live through a false self, he will immediately enter a cycle of continuous transition between regret, worry and out of body excitement, even if he does not notice it much. His mind will flutter between the past and the future. He is movement from busyness. When he chooses to be in oneness with himself, he becomes movement from stillness in the now.

Thus, Jesus discovered that we can know when we are living divine life. Further, we can experience it in others. It is not something spiritual that we must blindly believe in. It is not miracles worked by a person that makes him a saint. It is movement from stillness.

Today, some relaxation therapists and clergy teach people to move from stillness. They call the practice, "mindfulness," "non-thinking movement," "contemplation in action," and by many other terms. Of course, if people are taught to do it rather than live it by choosing to be their real selves, they will fail in those exercises.

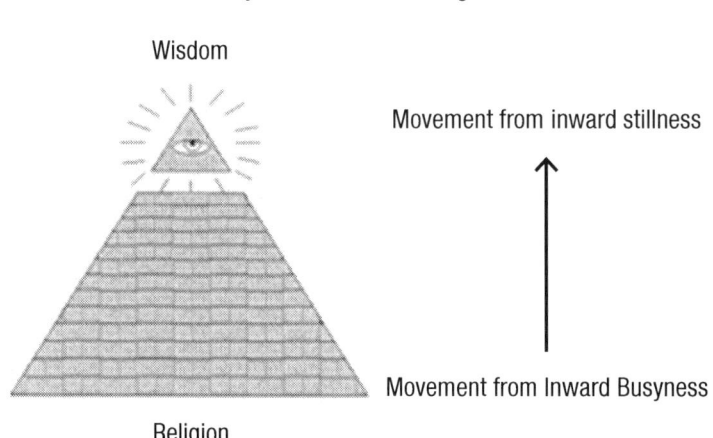

"We have come outward of the light." We are light.

Interestingly, Jesus never says that we are "outward of darkness." He never gives darkness such a power. He never talks about darkness as an intelligent source, such as Satan. He never explains an opposite to the light of the Father. Consequently, we know that he observed that the Father was the light in all, including darkness.

Instead, he observes that we are the source of darkness to the degree that we choose to not be our true selves. We are therefore, responsible for evil. He will not permit the attribution of evil to an imaginary outside source, such as Satan.

We were born with light. It is an intelligent power with the ability to choose. We use it to stand ourselves on our own true feet or on our false feet. Through this means, we choose to be good or bad, saints or sinners, light or darkness.

Ways of Wisdom and Religion

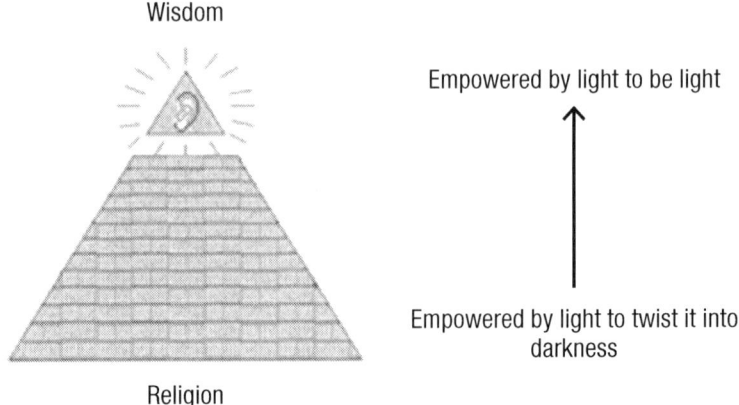

RECOGNIZE OUR TWO MOTHERS

Jesus discovered that we have two mothers (Poem Four, Chapter 20 (Saying 101)):

Jesus
said this:

My mother,

*She
brought me
forth,*[1]

*My Mother
however,*

The true,[2]

*She
gave to me
Life.*[3]

[1] *She brought me forth*: My physical mother "brought me" into many false selves.

[2] *The true*: My divine Mother.

[3] *She gave to me Life*: She gave me my core real, light, divine Life.

"My mother, she brought me forth." My mother who was not completely one with her true self, brought me forth to be like her.

Mary may have taught Jesus to identify with being a man, a Jew, a poor person, a tan person, and a brother to his siblings. Whenever he identified with any of those traditions, titles or roles, he identified with a false self. As he did that, he became divided from his true self and in the absence of light.

"My mother, the true, she gave to me Life." My divine mother not only shared her divine life with me, she made me aware that that is who I am. Therefore, forever I will seek to become single with that core life.

Jesus soul-knew that he was not his false selves. He had to discover for himself how to abandon them and become his true self.

"Father" "Mother": Jesus has now said that he experiences with soul-knowing two God-Persons in one. He called one Person, "Father," and the other "Mother." They are the source of the life and light within us, as he says.

We have all heard that the Israelites believed in one Lord. That is not true. The Bible begins with the following:

> *In the beginning*
> *Elohim*
> *created heaven*
> *and earth.*
>
> *(Gen. 1:1)*

Throughout the Old Testament, in particular in Genesis, the Hebrew word, "Elohim," has been translated, "Lord." However, "Elohim" is plural. It means "strong Ones" or "Gods." Jesus knew that, and when he looked at the obvious, that little children are male and female, he understood that the sources of life within us were both masculine and feminine. He called one, "Father," and the other, "Mother."

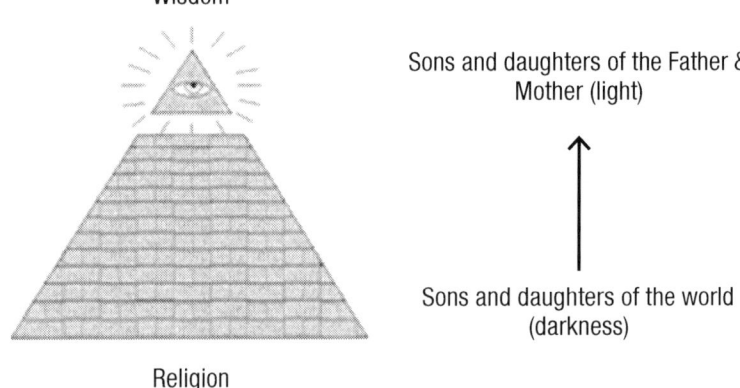

Jesus soul-knew that the Sons and daughters of the Father and Mother live out of a different life (Poem Five, in Chapter 21 (Saying 111a)):

> Jesus
> said this:
>
> *He,*
>
> *Who*
> *Lives[1]*
>
> *Out of He[2]*
>
> *Who*
> *lives,[3]*
>
> *Will peer*
> *not on death.[4]*

[1] *Lives*: Lives the life of our Father and Mother.

[2] *Out of He*: Out of the Father.

[3] *Who lives*: Who lives light in oneness with his true self.

[4] *Death*: Dividedness, movement from busyness.

Ways of Wisdom and Religion

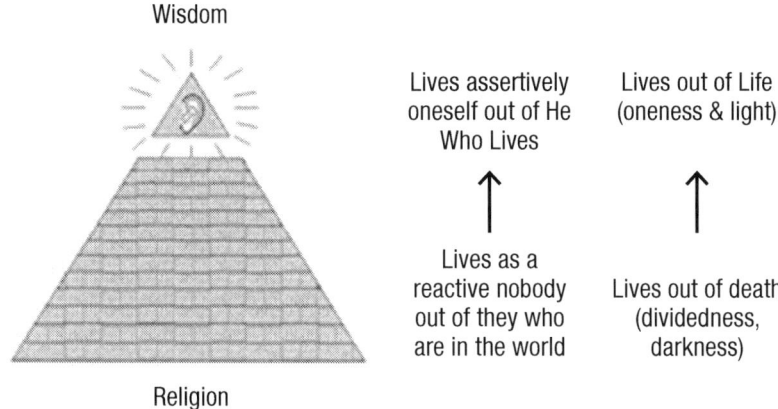

Become the All

When we live out of He Who Lives, we evolve naturally to be more our true selves and into oneness with all others. We cannot become our true selves without healing our dividedness from others. We cannot heal our dividedness from others without becoming one with ourselves. Both must be accomplished to live life out of He Who Lives. Jesus says this beautifully in Poem Ten, Chapter 16 (Saying 77):

Jesus
said this:
*I am
the light,*[1]

[1] *I am the light*: I am undivided and one with He Who Lives.

The One[2]

[2] *The One*: The divine Light.

*Which
is
upon them,*[3]

[3] *Which is upon them*: Which shows everyone the Way. Which is the salvation of the world.

All of them.[4]

*I
am
the all.*[5]

*Has
the All*[6]
*come outward
of me;*

*And
has
the all
split
to become me.*[7]

*Split
a timber*[8]

*And
I
am
there.*[9]

*Take
the stone*[10]
up,

*And
you
will discover me
there.*[11]

[4]*All of them*: All people, animals, plants and things.

[5]*I am the all*: I live the light and life that is in everything, even things that many regard as inanimate. It is all divine light and life.

[6]*Has the all come outward of me*: Has the divine light in all come from me.

[7]*Has the all split to become me*: Has the divine life in all become uniquely me.

[8]*Split a Timber*: Split a person's support. A house is like a person. A house is constructed of timbers and stones. A "timber" is a strong structural element.

[9]*Split a timber, And I am there*. Look inside the fundamental support of a person, and I am present.

[10]*Stone*: A word.

[11]*Take the stone up*: Look under what a person says, and you will find me.

"I am the all." I am the core life in everyone and everything.

Jesus grew to identify with nothing else.

"I am the light…I am the all." I am the light intelligence that is in all, guiding all to evolve.

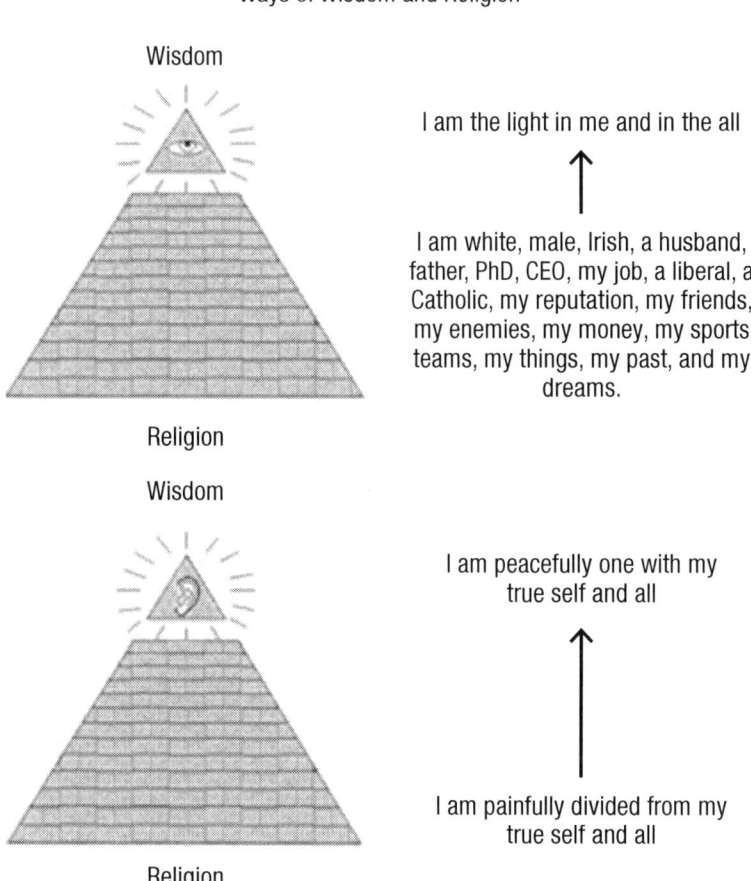

CHAPTER THREE

PAUL'S VIEW OF THE HUMAN CONDITION

PAUL REJECTS JESUS' WAY

Paul the Apostle created the foundation of the Christianity that we know today. He never met Jesus. He was a Jewish cleric who began arresting, persecuting, and killing the followers of Jesus shortly after Jesus's death. He never said why he was doing that; however, the author of the Acts of The Apostles (thought to be Luke the Evangelist), tells us that Paul (called "Saul" before he became a Christian) was trying to destroy Jesus' "Way:"

> *But Saul, still breathing threats and murder against the disciples of the Lord, went to the high priest and asked him for letters to the synagogues at Damascus, so that if he found any belonging to the Way, men or women, he might bring them bound to Jerusalem. (Acts 9: 1-2).*

For nearly two thousand years, people have speculated about the nature of the "Way" that so enraged Paul and his superiors.

After a few years of chasing down Christians, Saul had a conversion experience near Damascus in which he was told that Jesus was the expected Messiah. Instead of humbly returning to Jerusalem to study with Jesus' apostles and disciples, he traveled to Arabia to decide how to proceed. On the one hand, he was disturbed by this new Way of Jesus, and on the other, he knew that Jesus was the man he wished to follow. Those were huge problems he needed to resolve.

In Arabia, Saul changed his name to "Paul" and became inspired to think of himself as an apostle. He said of himself later in Gal. 1:1:

> *I, Paul an apostle, (not of men, neither by man, but by Jesus Christ, and God the Father).*

This tells us that Paul learned in a direct revelation that Jesus and the Father had commissioned him to be not a disciple of Jesus, but the 13th apostle.

Apparently, Paul had the revelation that Jesus wanted to replace the gospel that he had spent his life preaching and writing about with another gospel that would be revealed to him. He tells us in Gal. 1:11:

> *I want you to know, brothers and sisters, that the gospel I preached is not of human origin. I did not receive it from any man, nor was I taught it; rather, I received it by revelation from Jesus Christ.*

That is quite a statement. Paul wants himself and us to believe that Jesus, who Paul in other writings calls the "son of God," spent his entire life on earth preaching a gospel he regrets formulating. This perfect God-man now needed to correct himself through Paul.

With that revelation, Paul had justification for not going to Jerusalem and studying with the Apostles and the other disciples of Jesus. He needed not learn everything that Jesus taught because it was all wrong. Jesus, the all-knowing, all-perfect God, blew it. Paul believed that Jesus and the Father commissioned him to be humankind's savior from Jesus' own false message.

Jesus died in the year 30 CE. Paul began persecuting Christians shortly after Jesus's death. He had his conversion experience in about 37 CE. He was in Arabia from 37 or 38 CE until 40 CE, and died in 62CE.

Ways of Wisdom and Religion

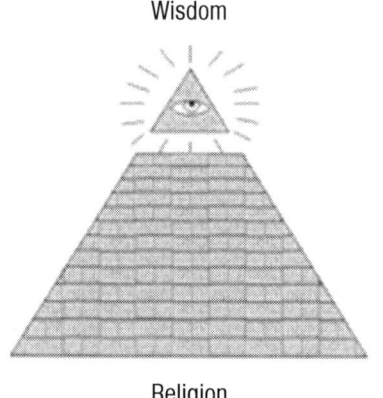

Wisdom

The Way of Wisdom that Jesus preached

The Way of Religion Paul preached as a replacement for the Way that Jesus preached

Religion

Paul's View of a Little Child

Paul decided that all of humankind's problems arose from his sinful nature. Jesus looked at a little child and saw life and Light. Paul saw death and darkness. He wrote in Romans 5: 12-13:

> *Sin entered the world through one man (Adam), and death through sin, and in this way death came to all people, because all sinned— To be sure, sin was in the world before the law was given, but sin is not charged against anyone's account where there is no law.*

"Sin entered the world through one man and death through sin." In the beginning, there was no sin and no physical death, instead, there was only spiritual and physical life. Because the sin of Adam is passed down through the patrilineal line, every person is born in sin that results in physical death.

Thus, we each may decide to agree with either Jesus or Paul about the nature of a little child.

Ways of Wisdom and Religion

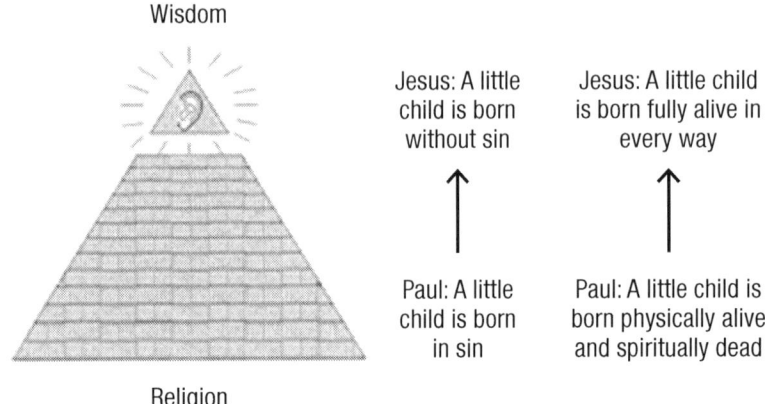

Jesus' and Man's Body

Jesus, according to Paul, possessed a body different from the body in people. He called it a "likeness." We read about that in Philippians 2: 5-10:

> *Christ Jesus, who, though he was in the form of God, did not count equality with God a thing to be grasped, but emptied himself, taking the form of a servant, being born in the likeness of men. And being found in human form he humbled himself and became obedient unto death, even death on a cross.*

"Christ Jesus who, though he was in the form of God, did not count equality with God a thing to be grasped, but emptied himself, taking the form of a servant, being born in the likeness of men." Jesus, the Messiah, was born as God without sin resulting in physical and spiritual death; however, because sinful man could not comprehend such magnificence, he took on the form of a human servant. He was not really in a sinful body that could physically die, but appeared to be in one.

"And being found in human form he humbled himself and became obedient unto death, even death on a cross." And when people saw his human form and hated him, he became obedient to them and let them murder his body on the cross; although, he, as a person, could not die.

Thus, Paul preached that Adam and Eve were born whole and perfect and immortal. However, after Adam sinned, his progeny possessed a sin that we know is there because humans die. That sin also accounts for all of the inner conflict within a person and all of the conflicts between people.

Paul says that Jesus, on the other hand, came into the world without inheriting sin in spirit or body. He was a man in form, but not in substance.

Ways of Wisdom and Religion

Wisdom

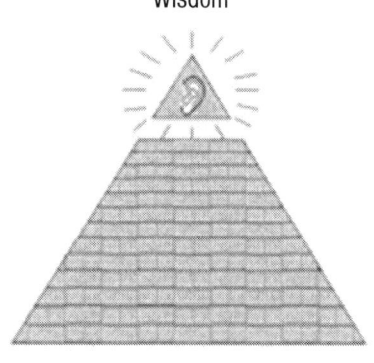

Jesus: I was born a little child with core light and life, just like everyone else

Paul: Jesus was born a little child in a body free of sin. People are born in sin in spirit and body

Religion

Paul's Belief in the Unseen

In 2 Cor. 4, Paul glorifies the fact that he and his followers based their life blindly believing in "things that are unseen:"

> *For this slight momentary affliction is preparing for us an eternal weight of glory beyond all comparison, because we look not to the things that are seen but to the things that are unseen; for the things that are seen are transient, but the things that are unseen are eternal.*

"For this slight momentary affliction is preparing for us an eternal weight of glory beyond all comparison, because we look not to the things that are seen but to the things that are unseen." This slight momentary affliction, from getting sick to being tortured and killed, prepares those who believe in the unseen to be glorified after we physically die.

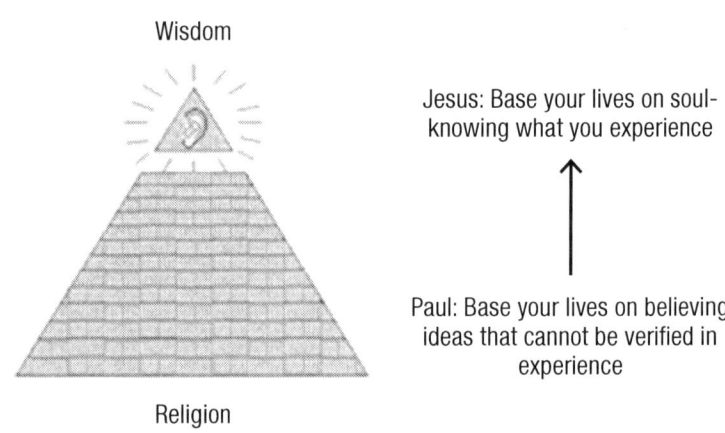

"For the things that are seen are transient, but the things that are unseen are eternal." The life you see in a little child, in a smile, in one who sacrifices for others, is not a manifestation of everlasting life. Instead, have faith in the primacy of the unseen.

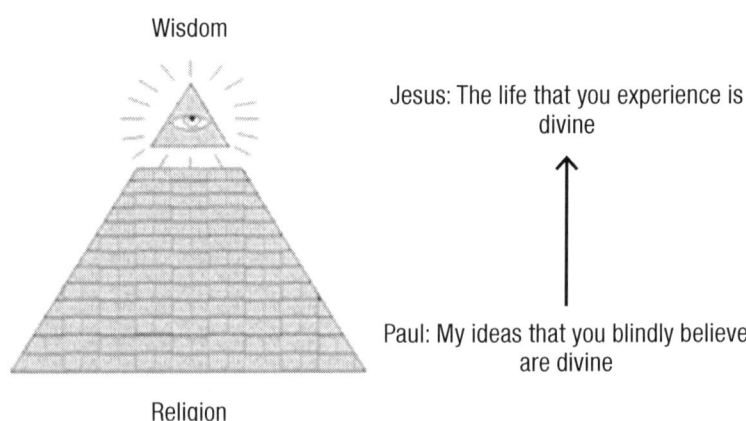

CHAPTER FOUR

THE GOALS OF JESUS' WAY OF WISDOM

Discover the Kingdom

In several previous poems, Jesus said that he discovered a "place of life" at our core. He also calls that place, the "kingdom." We see this in the following Poem One from Chapter 11 (Saying 49) where he summarizes the goal of the Way of Wisdom:

Those blessed ones,[1]

    They
    are
the single ones,[2]
    and
the chosen ones;[3]

    For
    you
will discover the kingdom;[4,5]

[1] *Blest ones*: Those who are full of light and divine life.

[2] *Single ones*: People congruent with their true nature.

[3] *Chosen ones*: The Father chose to give them congruence with their divine life.

[4] *Kingdom*: One's core, real, divine self.

[5] *You will discover the kingdom*: For you will rediscover the kingdom you were born with. We each are a unique manifestation of the kingdom. We can prevent it from manifesting itself.

For *you* *are out* *of it,*[6]	[6]*For you are out of it*: We all remember the kingdom that we really were when we were born; consequently, we all seek it behind every choice.
And again, *you* *will be going* *there.*[7]	[7]*Will be going there*: The kingdom is in us waiting.

"The blessed ones are the single ones...For you will discover the kingdom." The blessed ones grow to split their allegiance less and less between many false selves, and to become "single" with who they are. Therefore, they increasingly rediscover their true selves and their interactions with others.

Those blest ones evolve out of being nationalists, racists, and sexists. They evolve out of being separatists, elitists, isolationists, and patriots. They evolve toward singleness with the intelligence within all.

"For you are out of it." We all remember a life where we were wonderfully happy just being us and the all. Now, we experience worry, regret, mania, depression and longing. We ask, "What caused us to come to the point where we must struggle to find kingdom joy again?"

"And again you will be going there." And again, when you follow the Way of Wisdom, you choose to be the kingdom again.

Ways of Wisdom and Religion

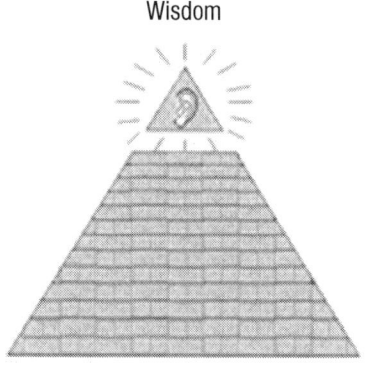

Wisdom

You leave the world to again become the wise ruler over yourself that you were at birth.

↑

You leave your incorrect and sinful Ways to lose yourself in the beliefs of those whom you admire in the world

Religion

An aside: Some may be asking, do we go into the kingdom once and for all, or do we move in and out? Let me explain my understanding with reference to a more modern Jewish theologian/philosopher, Martin Buber.

Buber stated that we can be in one of two kinds of relationships: One he called "I-Thou," the other, "I-It." The former is a genuine relationship fostered by a person who is congruent with himself. The latter is a manipulative relationship initiated by a person who is not himself. Buber also found that a person could not be in both at the same time; rather, one flipped from one to the other. If one wishes, he may develop himself to be gradually more I-Thou in every thought and action.

Jesus seems to have said something similar 2000 years ago. For Jesus, the kingdom includes an I-Thou relationship; however, as we have seen and will see, it is much more than that. He calls those in I-It relationships, "the world." His Way of Wisdom is the means by which we may grow to live in the kingdom all of the time.

Will of the Father

Those on the Way become one within and as a community because they get their orders from one source. Jesus tells us that in Chapter 19: Poem Four (Saying 99):

The disciples
said to him:

"Your brothers
and
your mother,[1]

They
are standing there,[2]

They
on the side
outward."[3]

He
said to them:

"Those
Who
are
in these places,[4]

Who
do the will
of my Father,[5]

They
are
my brothers
and
my mother.[6]

[1] *Your brothers and your mother*: The network of people tied to your Way of Religion (parents, peers, teachers, clergy) who gave you your false identity.

[2] *They are standing there*: They are standing there with the expectation that you will grow to share their world and their world view.

[3] *On the side outward*: On the side of the world, on the side of darkness, on the side of movement from busyness, on the side of the Ways of Religion.

[4] *Places*: Places of divine life.

[5] *Who do the will of my Father*: Who live according to their true natures.

[6] *They are my brothers and my mother*: They are our true support network. They encourage us to stand on our own feet no matter how nonconformist we become.

"Your brothers and your mother, they are standing there, they on the side outward." Your family put up obstacles to you being your real nature.

"Those who are in these places, who do the will of my Father." Those who live from their places of light, where they soul-sense the will of the Father.

Many Catholics believe that the will of the Father comes down through a succession of Popes to their local Bishop and through him to the local Pastor who tells them how to think and act. Protestants reject that notion and instead look to scripture for the will of the Father. Catholics think that a clergyman speaks objective, absolute truth. Protestants think that scripture tells them objective, absolute truth.

Jesus disagrees with both. He tells us that truth comes to each of us subjectively through soul-knowing. His followers may get the will from a Papal encyclical one day, from scripture the next, from a billboard the next, from a child the next, and directly from a sensed insight the next day. Everyone interprets what he hears and sees subjectively. No one personally experiences objective truth. As one leaves all to soul-know, he does so without bias.

"They are my brothers and my mother." They are my intimate family of non-conformist soul-seekers. From them I learn how to discover myself as the kingdom.

Ways of Wisdom and Religion

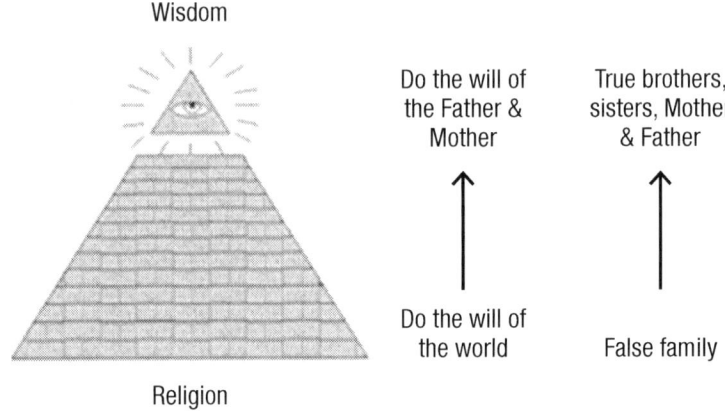

HATE YOUR FATHER AND MOTHER?

Jesus tells us that we all must sever our dependent relationships on the lives that our parents and authorities gave us and become one again with our real Mother and Father and with all in the kingdom. That is a very difficult process as Jesus points out in Poem Four, Chapter 20 (Saying 101):

Jesus said this:

Whoever hates his father, and his mother in my way not,[1]

Can come to be a disciple to me not.[2]

[1] *Whoever hates his father and his mother in my way not*: Whoever does not hate being the person he adopted when he identified with the beliefs, hopes, values and traditions of his parents, clergy, teachers, and other leaders.

[2] *Can come to be a disciple to me not*: Unless you stop identifying with your family life, you will not follow me, as I identify only with our Mother and Father and those brothers and sisters who do their will.

Ways of Wisdom and Religion

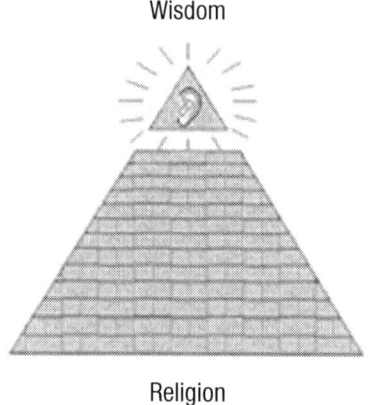

Wisdom

Hates the conformist messages given to him by his parents, friends, teachers, media and other leaders

Embraces the conformist messages given to him by his parents, friends, teachers, media and other leaders

Religion

LEAVE YOUR SEXUAL IDENTITY

Those on the Way of Wisdom must continually be on guard against the doctrines of the world that he adopted as he became socialized. Those doctrines are propagated by secular and theological authorities, oftentimes under the guise of so-called "common sense." For example, it is common sense to identify with masculinity or femininity and to assign roles, titles, and privileges to these false selves. We see that below in the clever Poem Eight of Chapter 21 (Saying 114):

Simon Peter said to him this: "Make Mary leave us, For women are worthy not of life."[1]	[1]*For women are worthy not of life*: For women are not worthy of life in the kingdom. When Jesus preached of life in the kingdom, his disciples interpreted him as meaning that women would be inferior in this new realm. They made this assumption because they adopted the "common sense" theological and secular beliefs in the inherent inferiority of women.

Jesus
said this:

"*Behold!*
I
myself
will lead her, ²

So that
I
might make her
male, ³

So that,
she
might come to be
a spirit ⁴

She
living ⁵

And
she
resembling
you males; ⁶

For
any woman,

Who
makes herself
male, ⁷

Will go
into the kingdom
of the heavens. ⁸

²*Lead her*: Empower her, teach her.

³*So that I might make her male*: So that I might show her how to identify with her core life and the identical core life in men. That I might teach her not to identify primarily with being a woman, which is a false self.

⁴*Spirit*: Her divine spirit.

⁵She *living*: She consciously identifying with the life of her Father and Mother in herself and all.

⁶She *resembling* you males: She possessing the core life just as males.

⁷*Makes herself male*: Who gives up her identification with her sexuality.

⁸*Kingdom of the heavens*: See below.

Evolve Through Heavens

We will return to that Poem about sexual stereotypes; however, to understand it, we need to analyze the strange last phrase, "kingdom of the heavens(pl)." Jesus defines an evolved Way of living as a kingdom made up of a number of heavens. Let us read the entire second part of the Poem again:

> *For*
> *any woman,*
>
> *Who*
> *makes herself*
> *male,*
>
> *Will go*
> *into the kingdom*
> *of the* **heavens**[(pl)].

First, Jesus defines kingdom in another way in Chapter Two, Poem Two (Saying 3):

> Jesus
> said this:
>
> *The kingdom,*
>
> *It*
> *is*
> *of your eye*[1]
> *inward,*[2]
>
> *And*
> *it*
> *is*
> *of your eye*
> *outward.*[3]

[1] *Eye*: Third eye.

[2] *It is of your eye inward*: It is a means of looking "inward" at yourself with your third eye.

[3] *It is of your eye outward*: It is a means of seeing outward with fresh eyes like seeing with the fresh eyes of a child.

Based on that Poem, Jesus tells us that a kingdom is a means by which one looks at himself inwardly and at the world outwardly. From previous poems, we also know that we were born with third-eye knowledge of all. We also know that we abandoned it for the world's two-eye seeing, and that to the degree that we evolve on the Way of Wisdom, we return to using only one-eye seeing.

In summary, we were born into the "kingdom" means of viewing ourselves, others, and the world. In that kingdom, we ruled ourselves differently than we do when we identify with false selves and their doctrines. We also know that to become that kingdom again, we must hate the false enculturation that we received from our families, friends, and teachers.

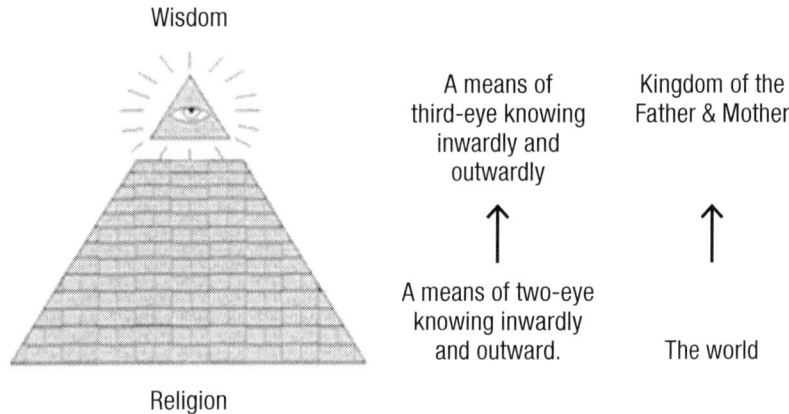

Jesus gives us more information about his meaning for "heavens" in Poem Three, Chapter Three (Saying 11):

Jesus said this:	[1]*Heaven*: A level of knowing oneself, others, and the world.
This heaven,[1]	
It will pass away;[2]	[2]*Pass away*: Our present level of knowing will pass away as we become more fully alive. Thus, our perception of truth changes as we evolve.
And the one above it,[3]	[3]*The one above it*: There are infinite levels of knowing or truth.
It will pass away.[4]	[4]*It will pass away*: Each level of knowing must be given up in order to reach a higher level of knowing.

"This heaven will pass away." This level of knowing inwardly and outwardly will pass away as one evolves. Thus, each level is a level of experiencing or being.

We can deduce from that Poem that the word "heaven" in Thomas does not mean a place that one goes to after he dies. That kind of heaven does not pass away. Nor does it refer to the place where God lives.

Heaven is a level of wisdom. As one grows, one passes through levels of heavens. For those who remain fixed in their steadfast faiths, their heavens will not "pass away."

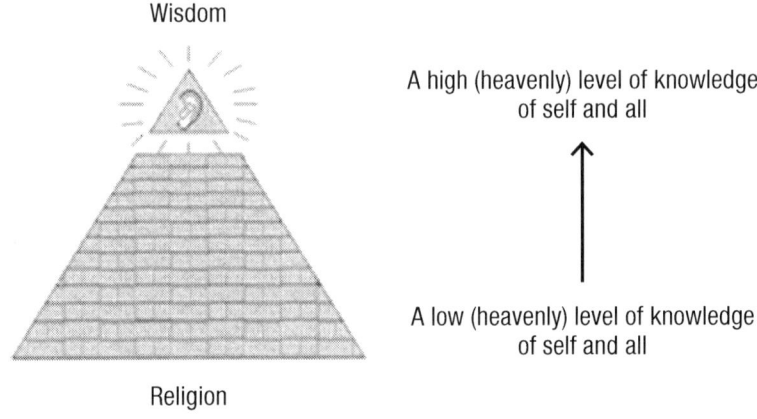

"And the one above it, it will pass away." And my heavenly level of beliefs above this level, it will dissolve as I evolve.

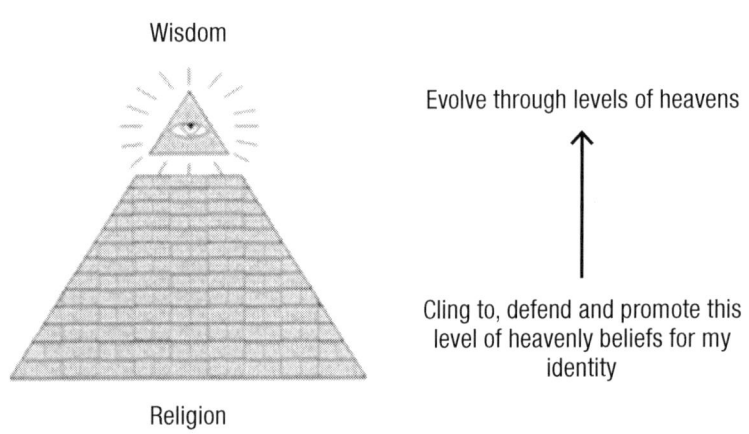

The wise also know to not identify with their current truth, because it isn't the entire picture.

The wise person will base his life on natural beliefs, those that he discovered in himself, in others, and in the world. The unwise will base his life on doctrines, usually those of others.

The wise understand the thinking of the unwise person; however, the unwise cannot understand the thinking of the wise person.

For the unwise person to be able to understand the wise person, he must evolve to the higher level of heavenly life and wisdom of the more evolved person.

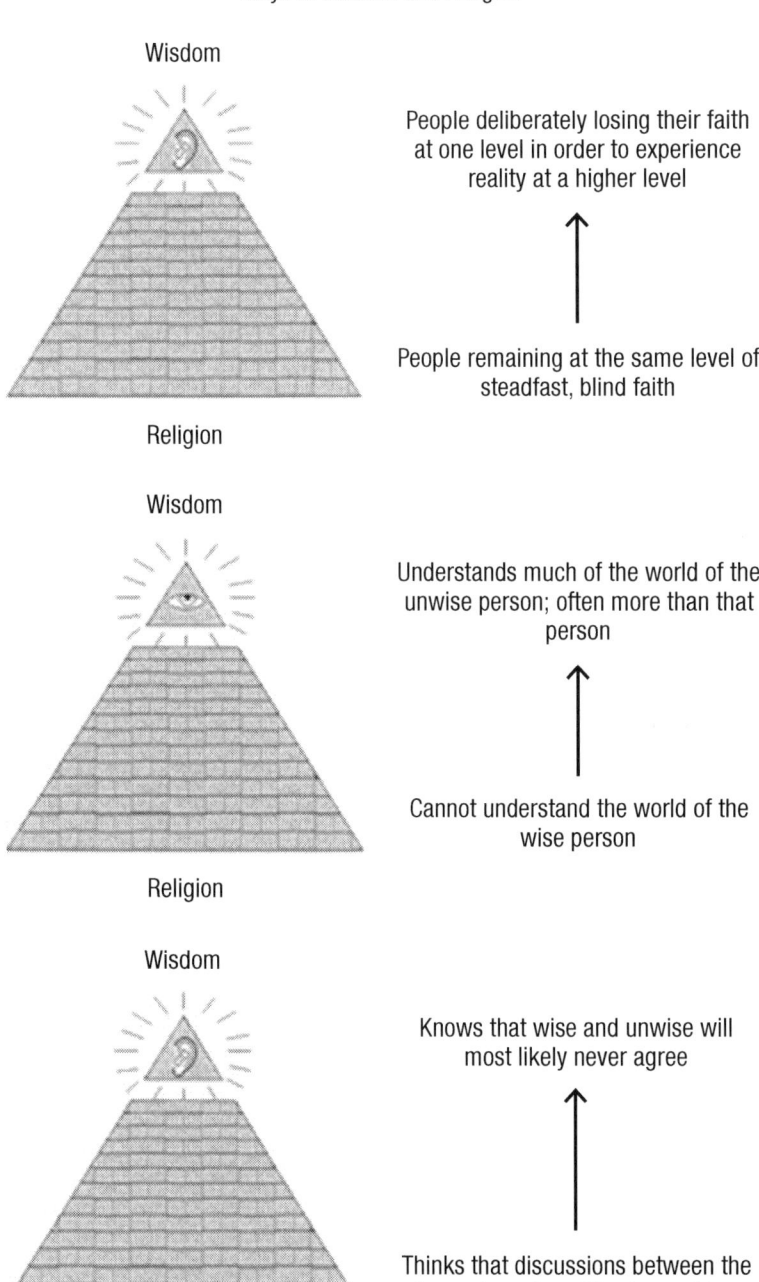

Those on the Way of Religion seek absolute truths. Those on the Way of Wisdom know that they will never know an absolute truth. They will get infinitely closer, but never reach it.

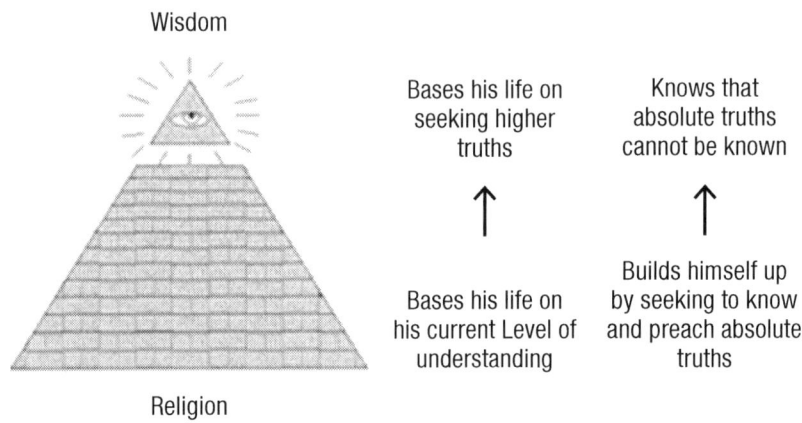

According to Jesus, as one grows on the Way of Wisdom, one undergoes changes in his perception. On the Way of Religion, one may live year after year without noticing any differences in the way he perceives himself or others. It's difficult for him to change because he develops habits of seeing things in one way, which prevents him from soul-seeing in another way. Thus, he becomes blind to new ways of looking at things. Further, that blindness prevents him from seeing how he nurtures his inner death.

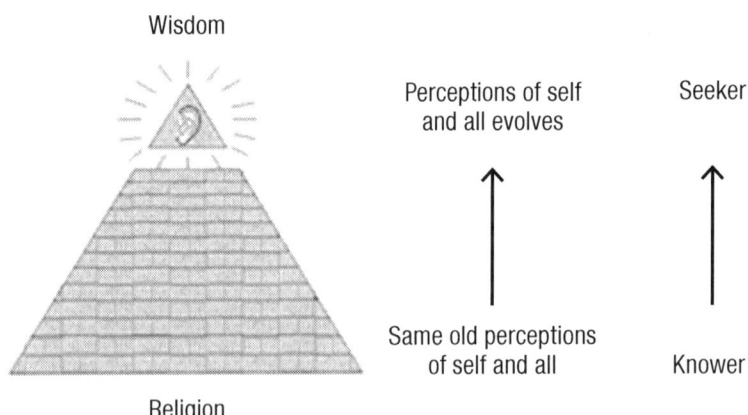

Evolve to Know Your Divinity

To know oneself as Jesus knew himself with his soul-knowing, one must pass upward through many levels of heaven. From a high level, Jesus exclaimed something most will find surprising, which we read in Chapter Two, Poem Five (Saying 3b):

Jesus
said this:

When
you
should know yourselves,[1]

Then,
they
will know you,[2]

And
you (pl.)
will realize[3]

That
you[(pl.)]
are
sons
of the Father[4]

Who
lives.[5]

If
you
will know yourselves
not,[6]

[1] *When you should know yourselves*: When you should soul-know yourselves at a high level of heaven.

[2] *Then they will know you*: Those living at low and high levels of heaven will know you. Those at a low level will know that you are different, but they will not understand the difference. Those living at a high level will know the real you.

[3] *And you will realize*: And you will realize from everyone's response to you.

[4] *You will realize that you are sons of the Father*: You all will soul-recognize your heritance from your divine Parents.

[5] *Who lives*: Who lives divine life.

[6] *If you will know yourselves not*: If you will not soul-know yourselves at a high level of heaven.

<table>
<tr><td>

Then

you

exist

in poverty,[7]

And

you

are

the poverty.[8]

</td><td>

[7]*Then, you exist in poverty.* You will be inwardly impoverished of that which you need in order to be fulfilled.

[8]*And you are the poverty:* You will be poorness itself. A void of life. Something that diminishes the world.

</td></tr>
</table>

"When you should know yourselves, then, they will know you." When you soul-know yourselves at a high level of heaven, then people will know that you are a kingdom.

"And you[(pl.)] **will realize that you**[(pl.)] **are sons of the Father who lives."** And you will realize humbly that you are sons and daughters of the Father who lives one with you.

"If you will know yourselves not." If you will insist that the self you know is all that there is to know. If you will not give up your present beliefs about yourself. If you want to live the life you live today forever.

"Then, you exist in poverty." You choose not to live a life of richness from the joy of the soul. You are instead seeking false riches from people who can offer you nothing truly satisfying.

"And you are the poverty." And you help destroy the world.

The Goals of Jesus' Way of Wisdom

Ways of Wisdom and Religion

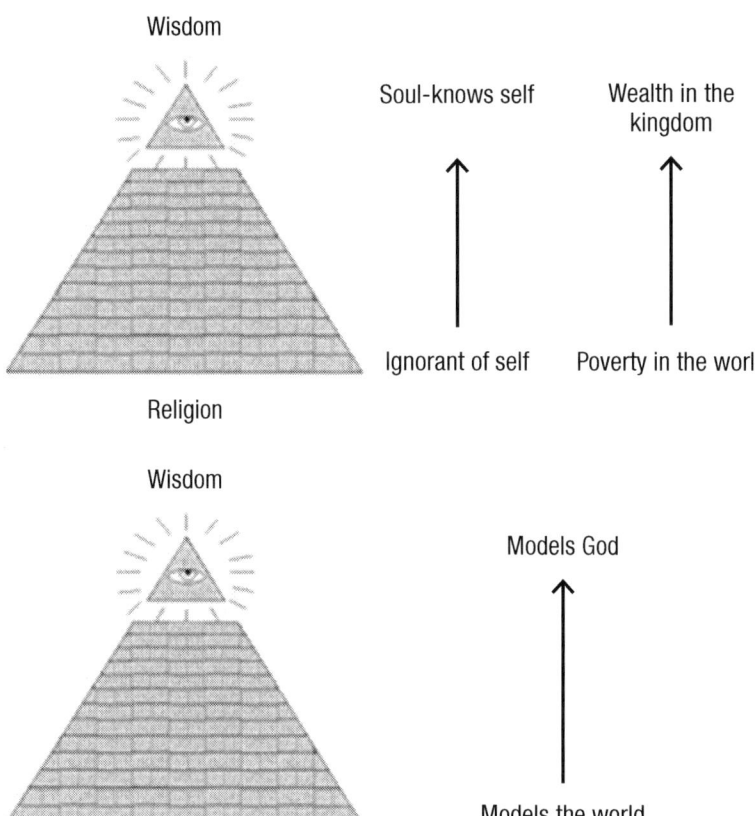

Be a Twin

Now we are ready to further analyze Poem Eight of Chapter 21 (Saying 114). Notice the Poem's shift in tone:

> Simon Peter
> said to him
> this:
>
> "Make Mary
> leave us,
>
> For
> women
> are
> worthy not
> of the life."
>
> Jesus
> said this:
>
> "Behold!
> I
> myself
> will lead her,
>
> So that
> I
> might make her
> male,
>
> So that,
> she
> might come to be
> a spirit
>
> She
> living

And
she
resembling
you males;

For
any woman,

Who
makes herself
male,

Will go
into the kingdom
of the heavens."

Peter says: **"Make Mary leave us, for women are worthy not of the life."** Look Jesus, were you not taught God's order: that women need to humbly accept their essential inferiority in life? We are not threatened by them, and it is not that they are not good people. However, notice, God raised up Abraham and Moses, both men. By doing that, God declared that men are the superior, naturally more alive, wise leaders that the world needs. Therefore, for the sake of our traditions, our society, common sense, and these women, make Mary leave us.

Ways of Wisdom and Religion

Wisdom

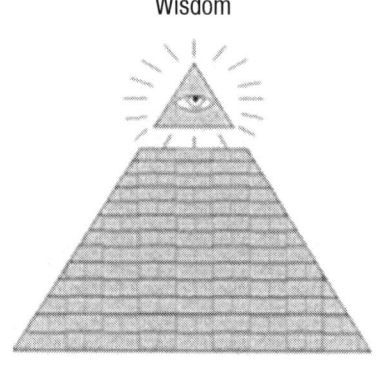

Brings light and disruption to the discriminative tendencies of the world

Supports and defends the discriminative tendencies of the world

Religion

Jesus says: **"Behold! I myself will lead her."** Look Peter, I will lead her to become more of what she is.

"So that I might make her male." So that I might help her to reclaim her core life that is identical to that in every man.

"So that she might come to be a spirit, she living, and she resembling you males." So that she might identify with her core spirit, which is her unique version of the divine spirit in everyone; and thus, become a fraternal twin of everyone.

"For any woman who makes herself male will go into the kingdom of the heavens." For any woman who becomes the twin of the core, divine life in men will rule wisely at a high level of heaven. Further, any woman who does not identify with the core life in all men, and any man who does not identify with the core life in all women, will devolve in misery to a low level of worldly ignorance and death.

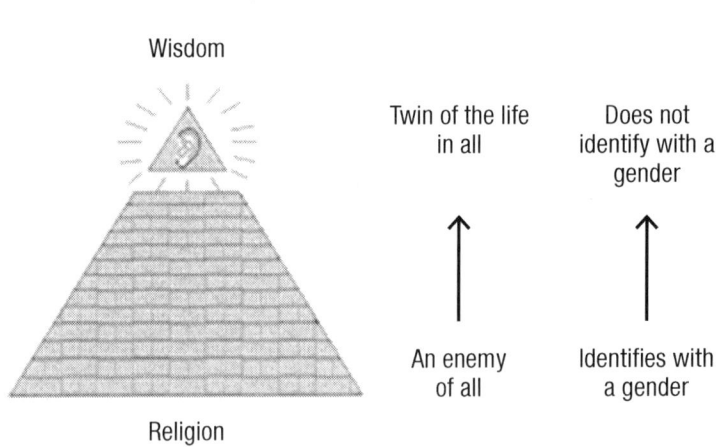

Ways of Wisdom and Religion

Be a Lion

As we see in the above Poem, Jesus is not the all-loving Jesus that many imagine. He is a lion who eats his enemies, like Peter, alive. Let us read about that lion in Chapter Two, Poem Seven (Saying 7):

Jesus
said this:

A blessed one,[1]

He
is
the lion,[2]

The one,

That
the man[3]
will eat,[4]

And
the lion
comes to be
the man.[5]

And
he
is cursed,[6]

Namely
the man,[7]
The one,

Whom
the lion
will eat,[8]

[1] *A Blessed one*: A person evolved in wisdom and life at a high level of heaven.

[2] *Lion*: A person who is not naïve like a child. He guards his aliveness and attacks those following the Way of Religion who are a threat.

[3] *Man*: A seeker of the life and wisdom of the lion.

[4] *Eat*: Takes in the wisdom of the lion, digests it, implements it, and makes it part of his life in his own fashion.

[5] And the *Lion comes to be the man*: And the wisdom of the lion comes to be the life and wisdom of the seeker.

[6] *Cursed*: Alive-dead..

[7] *Man*: A person who seeks to be a conformist to people-think rather than to be congruent with himself and one with all. A person who identifies with society's expectations and not with his core life.

[8] *Whom the lion will eat*: The lion sees the death in a man and destroys him with a word or glance—as Jesus did to Peter in the previous Poem. In that way, he eats him alive.

And the lion comes to be the man.[9]

[9] *And the lion comes to be the man*: The man becomes haunted by the memory of a lion who is so powerful, wise, and vigilant.
With the encounter with Jesus to Peter.
  Without the encounter with Jesus would have remained peacefully arrogant, blind and deaf. Instead, his false self was disrupted and he was forced to evolve or devolve.

"A blessed one, he is the lion." One blessed by being the divine presence in the world is a lion.

"The one that the man will eat." The lion whom a seeker of life listens to and models.

"And the lion comes to be the man." And the spirit of lion comes to be a similar spirit in the seeker.

"And he is cursed, namely the man, the one whom the lion will eat." And the non-seeker of life is cursed, because his pretenses of wisdom will be exposed and shredded by the wise lion.

"And the lion comes to be the man." And the way that the lion guarded himself and attacked the non-seeker's false identities will forever haunt the terrified victim.

The Goals of Jesus' Way of Wisdom

Ways of Wisdom and Religion

Wisdom

Religion

 Seekers humbly and hungrily eating the spirits of those more wise and alive

↑

Non-seekers haughtily distaining to learn from one more wise and alive

Wisdom

Religion

 A wise lion guarding and attacking his own false selves and those in others

↑

A boisterous mouse guarding and attacking threats to his false selves

Wisdom

Religion

 One possesses both childlike singleness and the wisdom and courage of a lion

↑

One is both duplicitousness and fearful

Ways of Wisdom and Religion

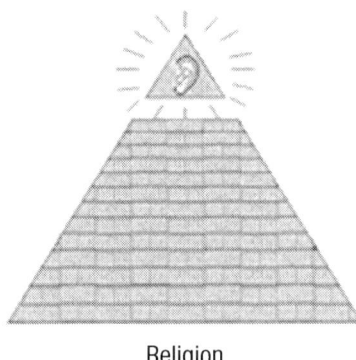

Wisdom

Jesus the lion: Humbly united with his true self and his brothers & sisters while guarding against threats to them

Peter the mouse: Proudly divided from himself and others

Religion

LOVE-GUARD

In Chapter Eight, Poem Five (Saying 25) Jesus explains how a child/lion encounters everyone and everything in the world:

Jesus
said this:

Love your brother[1,2]

*Like
your soul.*[3]

Guard him[4]

*Like
the pupil*[5]
of your eye.[6]

[1]*Brother*: One who possesses divine life. Every person, animal, plant and thing—all.

[2]*Love your brother*: Be in your heart place, a twin of all.

[3]*Soul*: Your unique essence. We are all unique essences of one divine life.

[4]*Guard him*: Protect and attack threats to your brothers.

[5]*Pupil*: Core.

[6]*Eye*: Third eye.

"Love your brother." Love the core life in people, plants, animals, and things.

"Love your brother like your soul." Unconditionally love your brothers for who they are, not for their false selves.

"Guard him." Protect yourself and your brothers from those not loving them unconditionally for who they are.

"Like the pupil of your eye." Like your most valuable possession, soul-knowing, without which, you cannot evolve.

Ways of Wisdom and Religion

Wisdom

Guard everyone from those who do not unconditionally love their core, divine life

↑

Guard people like yourself from people unlike yourself

Religion

Jesus loved the core light in Peter; however, he guarded himself and all people when Peter attacked a woman:

> Simon Peter
> said to him
> this:
>
> *"Make Mary
> leave us,*
>
> *For
> women
> are
> worthy not
> of life."*

"For women are worthy not of life." For one's sex determines one's worth on the Way of Religion. For half of the world are inherently inferior to me. For I need to be above women to feel good about myself. For women do not possess a soul like mine.

For his love of Peter and all people, Jesus guarded by saying:

"Behold!

I
myself
will lead her,

So that
I
might make her
male,

So that,
she
might come to be
a spirit

She
living

And
she
resembling
you males;

For
any woman,

Who
makes herself
male,

Will go
into the kingdom
of the heavens.

"Behold, I myself will lead her." Behold Peter and you other arrogant men, I will show you how wrong you are. I will become one with Mary in order to be her guide.

"So that I might make her male." So that she might stop identifying with what society has conditioned her to believe about her sex.

"So that, she might come to be a spirit, she living, and she resembling you males." So that she may become a twin in her spirit to all men and women.

That is quite an undertaking. To accomplish it, Jesus must teach Mary that a naïve lover loves everyone unconditionally. A follower of him loves everyone unconditionally for their core spirit and makes the tremendous effort to notice every flaw. Then, he guards himself and every other person, animal, plant and thing from the darkness he finds in another. In other words, everyone is loveable; however, everyone is dangerous to the degree that he has not evolved on the Way of Wisdom.

So, to evolve, Mary must become a child/lion who love-guards everyone that others dismiss. According to Jesus, there is no other means by which one may become fulfilled, sane, and wise.

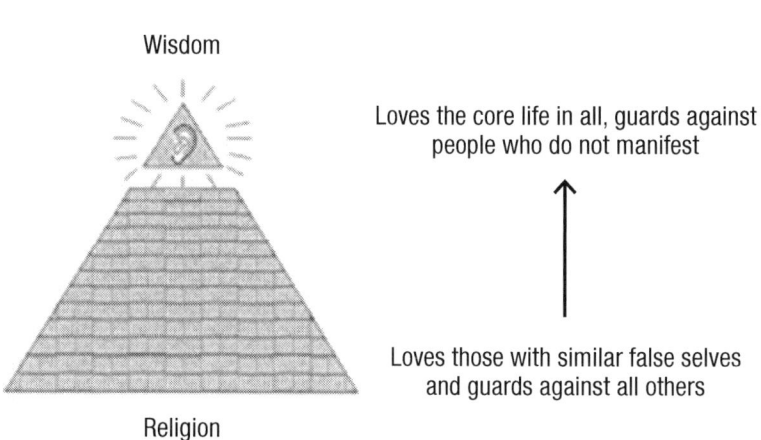

Ways of Wisdom and Religion

Be Cunning and Innocent

Jesus showed us that a fully alive person does the seemingly impossible, he unconditionally loves another; then, with the information that that love discloses, he cunningly guards himself and others. Jesus tells us that in Chapter 10, Poem One (Saying 39):

Jesus said this:	[1]*Come to be cunning*: Come to be cleverly guarding.
Come to be cunning like serpents.[1,2]	[2]*Serpent*: Jesus refers to the serpent in the Garden of Eden who cleverly seduced Eve.
And innocent like doves.[3]	[3]*And innocent like doves*: A dove is a symbol of inspiration. It gives us information when we become vulnerable.

"Come to be cunning like serpents." Discriminate light from darkness; use your cunning to guard yourself and your brothers and sisters.

"And innocent like doves." Be vulnerable and open to soul-know the essence of everyone beneath their false selves.

This is a dangerous world. Love and guard. Do not just love and fail to see the darkness.

Ways of Wisdom and Religion

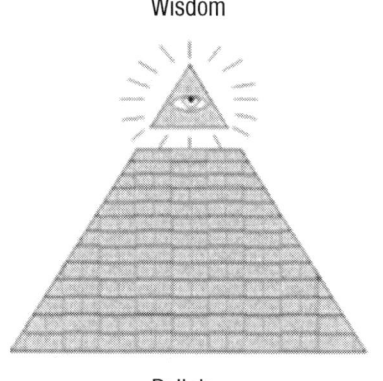

Wisdom

Uses innocence to love the light-life essence in all, and cunning to guard it

Uses ego to love and cunning to guard the dark-life in supporters.

Religion

To guard is to disrupt. Jesus expressed that in the following Poem Two from Chapter Four (Saying 16):

Jesus
said this:

Perhaps
they
are thinking,

Namely
men,[1]

That
I
have come
to throw peace
upon the world;[2]

[1] *Men*: People on the Way of Religion.

[2] *To throw peace upon the world*: To speak words to make those on the Way of Religion comfortable.

And
they
know
not

That
I
have come,
to throw divisions³
upon the earth:⁴,⁵

Fire,⁶
sword,⁷
and
war.⁸

For
there
are
five

Who
will come to be
in a house.⁹

There
are
three¹⁰
Who
will come to be
against two;

³*To throw divisions*: To cast words that expose an individual's incongruence with who he really is.

⁴*Earth*: Reflective consciousness.

⁵*Throw divisions upon the earth*: Say things that make the person reflect upon his duplicity, that is, that he is both a false and a real self.

⁶*Fire*: Words that burn one's conscience.

⁷*Sword*: Words that divide a person within, and that divide him from others.

⁸*War*: Words that cause 1) a person to fight himself, 2) people within a Way of Religion to fight one another, and 3) cause people on the two Ways to confront each other.

⁹*Five who will come to be in a house*: A "house" is primarily a person, and secondarily, a family or group. Jesus refers to one real person and four false persons within a single person, or five people in a family, one real and four false.

¹⁰*Three*: Three parts of oneself, or three persons in a family or group.

And
two
against three;[11]

The father[12]
against the son;[13]

And
the son
against the father;[14]

And
they
will stand on their feet;[15]

They
being
single ones.[16]

[11]*There are three who will come to be against two, and two against three*: There are three people on the Way of Wisdom who will come against two on the Way of Religion, and Two on the Way of Wisdom who will come against three on the Way of Religion.

[12]*Father*: Within each person and each group is a father personality who takes charge of passing on traditions.

[13]*Son*: Within each person and each group is a son personality who inherits the father's traditions.

[14]*The father against the son and the son against the father*: When the father and son are on different Ways, they will go "against" each other.

[15]*Stand on their feet*: Be confident in who they are, while the rest are shaken.

[16]*Single Ones*: People congruent with themselves.

Ways of Wisdom and Religion

Wisdom

Comforts those on the Way of Wisdom, disrupts the lives of those on Ways of Religion

↑

Comforts those on the same Ways of Religion, disrupts the lives of those on opposing Ways of Religion and Wisdom

Religion

Summary

- We know that the will of the Father and Mother is that you:

- Leave the Ways of Religion and evolve on the Way of Wisdom

- Soul-know yourself and all.

- Become congruent with oneself.

- Become innocent like a little child and a dove.

- Become a guarding, attacking lion.

- Stop identifying with your false identities.

- Hate your identification with the identities given to you by your parents, teachers, clergy and other leaders.

- Love-Guard all.

- Live from He Who Lives.

- Do the will of God.

- Disrupt your life and that of others to the degree that it reflects the Way of Religion.

CHAPTER FIVE

PAUL'S GOALS

Paul's Overall Plan

We left off with Paul in Arabia. There, he decided that a person was born with original sin and separated from God. Therefore, he had to decide if it was possible to unite that person with God again. He must have thought, "Perhaps mankind is doomed."

His revelation on the road to Damascus that Jesus was the Messiah told him that somehow Jesus was sent to save mankind from Adam's disobedience. However, Paul had several problems. First, Jesus never said he was the Messiah. Second, Jesus did not do the things that the Messiah was supposed to do, such as drive out the occupiers and bring everyone in the world to worship the one God of Israel. Nor did he cleanse the Temple and restore true Temple worship. Third, Jesus never said that he wanted to save humankind from original sin. Instead, Jesus preached a Way that Paul detested and that he probably knew would lead to the destruction of Judaism, to the raising of revolutionaries who would destroy all order, and because of original sin, to a world of unfettered debauchery.

So somehow, Paul needed to replace Jesus's Way, make it possible for people to be united with God again, show that Jesus was the Christ who was needed to save mankind, and form a church that would indoctrinate people to think and act in accord with Paul's interpretation of God's will. He probably, also possessed unconscious selfish desires to build up his own ego and remove all of his guilt about persecuting and killing followers of Jesus.

That would be an impossible agenda for most people, but not for Paul, the religious, murderous fanatic.

Blot Out Jesus' Gospel

He tackled the problem of erasing Jesus' Way easily. He decided to remove the real Jesus from the historical record by never quoting him.

Can we imagine that? He has never met Jesus, he knows that Jesus has a large following, he knows that people have memorized Jesus' wisdom poems, he is filled with love for the man who visited him in a vision; and yet, he decides that he will dedicate himself to destroying any written or memorized record of what Jesus said. Is that a plan that we would expect from someone of great character, or of a crazed fanatic?

As we know now, Paul largely succeeded! He never quotes any of Jesus' wisdom poems in any of his letters, and almost certainly never in any of his conversations. In other words, he deliberately hid Jesus' life's work: all of his parables, poems and sayings; and yet, claimed to be following the man.

Was Paul dishonest, delusional, or so unconscious that he believed his own lies?

Ways of Wisdom and Religion

Wisdom

Honestly agrees and disagrees with Jesus' gospel

Dishonestly disagrees with Jesus' gospel and hides it.

Religion

Declare that Jesus is God

The second thing Paul did was to decide that God still loved humans and wanted to unite them with himself. He believed that a man with original sin could not just say, "I'm sorry," and be welcomed by God to his former sonship. No, Paul believed the slap that Adam gave god was so grave that only another God could somehow make up for the affront. Further, that other God would have to do so in a way that necessitated the total submission of humankind to God's will.

Where was this other God? Paul decided that it was Jesus, despite the fact that Jesus never said that he was the only son of God. We read this in Paul's Letter to the Romans 1:1-4:

> *Paul, a servant of Jesus Christ, called to be an apostle, set apart for the gospel of God which he promised beforehand through his prophets in the holy scriptures, the gospel concerning his Son, who was descended from David according to the flesh and designated Son of God in power according to the Spirit of holiness by his resurrection from the dead.*

"Paul, an apostle of Jesus Christ, called to be an apostle, set apart for the gospel of God." I, Paul, called to be an apostle of Jesus, not by Jesus, but by God in a mystical vision, the one set apart from everyone in the world, including Jesus' disciples, to preach my gospel, which I call, "the gospel of God" to distinguish it from the gospel of Jesus.

Ways of Wisdom and Religion

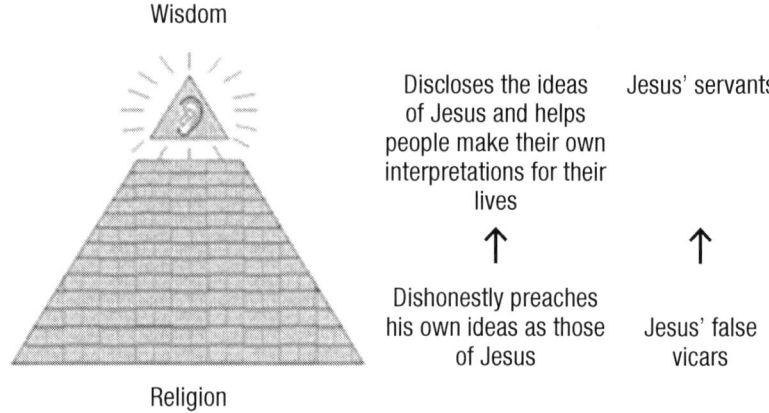

Discloses the ideas of Jesus and helps people make their own interpretations for their lives	Jesus' servants
↑	↑
Dishonestly preaches his own ideas as those of Jesus	Jesus' false vicars

"The gospel concerning his Son" My (Paul's) gospel concerning Jesus, who I declare to possess divine life, a life different from what we see in other humans, animals and plants.

Ways of Wisdom and Religion

Divine life in all
↑
|
Divine life in Jesus, which is radically different than the life in humans, plants, animals and everything else

"Who was descended from David according to the flesh and designated Son of God in power according to the Spirit of holiness by his resurrection from the dead." Jesus was biologically related to King David. When he was resurrected, the Holy Spirit showed everyone that 1) Jesus is the Son of God in a way that we are not, and 2) he was resurrected in a way that we cannot.

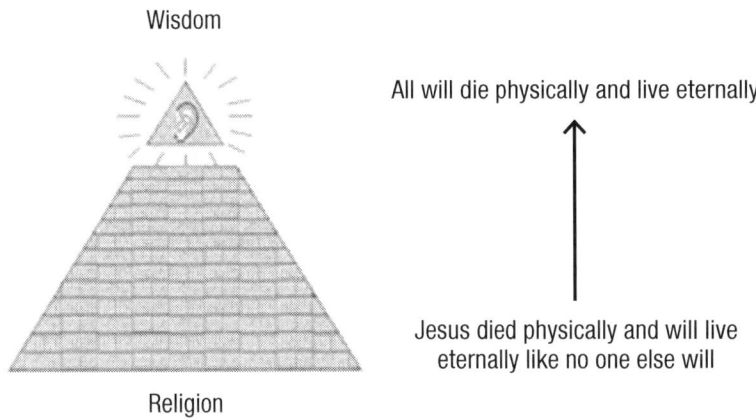

DECLARE THAT JESUS DIED FOR HUMANKIND'S SINS

Once Paul decided that Jesus had been designated "son of God" because he resurrected himself, Paul decided that Jesus sacrificed himself on the cross for humankind, even though Jesus never said that. In Romans 5: 10, we read:

> *For God has done what the law, weakened by the flesh, could not do: sending his own Son in the likeness of sinful flesh and for sin, he condemned sin in the flesh, (Rom. 8:1)*

"For God has done what the law, weakened by the flesh, could not." In other words, after God gave the laws to save humankind, God realized that those laws did not do what He thought they would do. God failed.

"God…sending his own Son in the likeness of sinful flesh and for sin, he condemned sin in the flesh." God sent his own Son not in human sinful flesh, but in flesh that looked like sinful flesh, and because he showed the difference between the two fleshes, he condemned the one that encases humans.

Ways of Wisdom and Religion

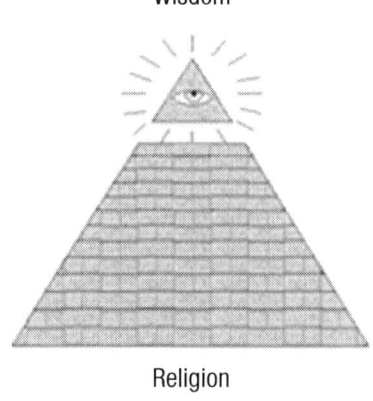

Paul goes on to say:

> *For if while we were enemies we were reconciled to God by the death of his Son, much more, now that we are reconciled, shall we be saved by his life. (Rom. 5:10)*
>
> *Christ loved us and gave himself up for us, a fragrant offering and sacrifice to God (Ephesians 5:2).*

"For if while we were enemies we were reconciled to God by the death of his Son." For while most humans did not regard God as their enemy, God declared them to be His enemy. However, God did not want them to be enemies; so He lovingly sent his Son to die a horrible death.

"Much more, now that we are reconciled, shall we be saved by his life." So now that God called us, "enemies" and figured out a means for us to be friends, we still needed to be "saved" from our sinful flesh by the special kind of life that Jesus lived. It was not enough that Jesus died, we must now do something else.

"Christ loved us and gave himself up for us, a fragrant offering and sacrifice to God." You see, the Messiah loved us and sacrificed his life as an offering to the God who declared us his enemies; so that God would feel differently about us.

Declare that People Need to Believe Paul's Gospel

However, Paul reasoned that it was not enough that Jesus died for the sins of humankind. People also had to agree to that.

Paul explains below that while everyone has been "reconciled," only those who believe that he has been reconciled by Jesus' death and resurrection would be "saved."

> *I (Paul) am making known to you, indeed, brothers, the gospel which I declared to you, which you received, and in which you also stand, by which you are saved, if you hold it fast, unless you believed in vain. For I delivered to you as of first importance what I also received: that Christ died for our sins in accordance with the scriptures, that he was buried, and that he was raised on the third day in accordance with the scriptures (1Cor. 15:34).*

In that quote, we find the four foundation stones of Paul's gospel and future church that he said was revealed to him in Arabia:

1. Christ died for our sins.

2. Christ was buried.

3. Christ was raised.

4. No one is "saved" unless he believes 1, 2 and 3.

Notice especially, belief number four: To be saved, to live forever with God, one must believe Paul's gospel, which he arrived at in mystical experiences. That justifies the need for Paul to start a hierarchical church that would both teach people to believe in his ideas, and convince them about their eternal reward and punishment if they did not. That also satisfied Paul's ego needs by putting him in the center of the church with his misrepresentation of Jesus.

It also ensured that he could be without guilt. He only needed to believe in his own beliefs to be forgiven by God. There was no need to ask forgiveness of the families he terrorized when he persecuted and killed their members. (Is that the thinking of a man of character?)

Declare that Jesus was the Messiah

Therefore, Paul proved to himself that Jesus really was the Messiah who came to drive out the occupiers of Israel, to cleanse the temple and to bring people to worship the one God of Israel. The Temple was our sinful flesh, which got cleansed so that we, the occupiers of it, could be saved when we believed that Jesus died for our sins.

Found a Religion to Indoctrinate People

However, Paul could not accomplish his mission unless he could establish a church and get people to believe him. That need forced him after three years to leave Arabia and return to Jerusalem (Galatians 1:18-24).

> *Then after three years, I went up to Jerusalem to get acquainted with Peter and stayed with him fifteen days. I saw none of the other apostles—only James, the Lord's brother. I assure you before God that what I am writing you is no lie.*

He met with James, the brother of Jesus and the head of the Jerusalem community, and with Peter, his assistant. We can only imagine their initial fear when he walked into the room; and then, their shock when he said he was preaching Jesus; and then, their total dismay when he laid out a gospel that they had never heard Jesus speak; and then, their complete shock when he told them that unless they abandoned Jesus' gospel and believed his, they would be eternally damned. James and Peter must have thought that they had died and been reborn in a house of warped mirrors.

Notice that Paul does not say that while in Jerusalem he visited the families of those he persecuted and killed. He never apologized for persecuting and killing the fathers and mothers of the children in the Jerusalem community. In his mind, he need not do that because he has been reconciled by Jesus' death and resurrection and self-saved by his belief in his own heard-from-God gospel.

The man remains in his heart a disassociated, depraved man, not unlike a man who has beat up his wife and returns, not to say, "I'm sorry," but to say, "I have changed." Like that man also, Paul actually wanted people to believe in him. (As history has shown, like in dysfunctional families, people have overlooked what Paul actually did and have believed him).

It would be an understatement to say that the meeting did not go well. After 15 days, Paul left to preach to Roman Gentiles, recognizing that Jews in Palestine would never believe him. It was 10 years before he returned to Jerusalem again.

Ways of Wisdom and Religion

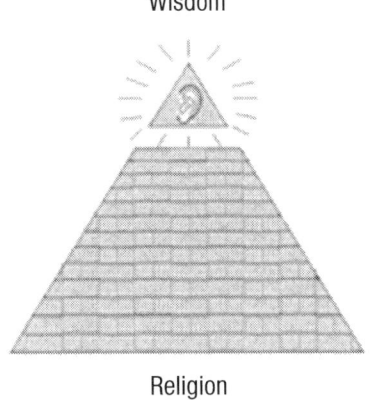

Wisdom

Religion

People are inherently fully alive, pure, wonderful, magnificent, beautiful, wise, divine beings

People are evil unless they believe in Paul's gospel

CHAPTER SIX

JESUS' SELF-DEVELOPMENT METHOD

Discover Yourself on Your Own

Jesus' message in the Gospel of Thomas leads to his summation in Chapter 21, Poem Six (Saying 11b)

Jesus said this: Whoever discovers himself on his own,[1] The world[2] is worthy of him not.	[1]Whoever discovers himself on his own: Whoever leaves indoctrinators (clergy, political leaders, parents, family, peers, professors, authors, the media, and all of his previous beliefs) and uses soul-knowing to discover himself on his own. [2]The world: Those on the Way of Religion.

"Whoever discovers himself on his own." Whoever uses soul-knowing to obtain the answers tailored to his specific history, and situation. Whoever leaves all to discover the all. Whoever is a rebel seeker.

Ways of Wisdom and Religion

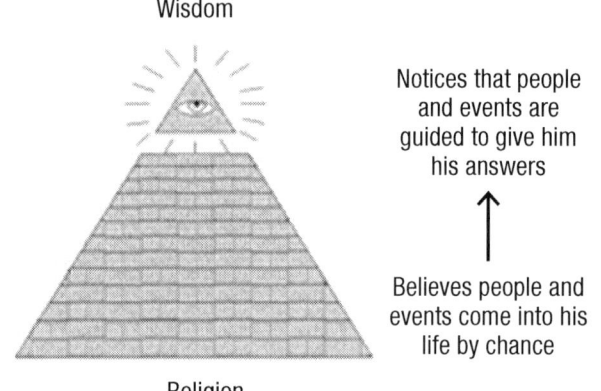

MAKE THE RIGHT FUNDAMENTAL CHOICE

One cannot be on the Way of Wisdom and the Way of Religion at the same time. Every choice we make determines which Way we follow. Jesus says in Poem Two, Chapter 11 (Saying 47):

Jesus
said this:

*In no way
can
a man
climb onto horses
two*[1]

*And
he
stretch bows
two.*[2]

[1] *Horses two*: A horse represents power. Within us are two powers. One from Light and the other from the dark self we create.

[2] *Stretch bows two*: A bow is strong intention. Within us is the intention to live more life or to live death.

In no way, *can* *a servant* *serve lords two;*³	³*Lords two*: Within us are two kinds leaders. Our divine Father and Mother is one. Way of Religion authorities is the other. Our Parents guide us continually through soul-knowing to be more ourselves. Our religious leaders tell us how to be fulfilled by being more false like them.
Or, *he* *will honor the one,*	
And *the other one,*	
He *will despise.*	

"In no way can a man climb onto horses two:" We ride power or self-confidence (a horse) in the world in only two Ways: On the Way of Wisdom or on the Way of Religion. We never straddle the two Ways. We live on one horse or the other.

For example, when we identity with a country, we identify with a brand of nationalism and its doctrine that includes a set of beliefs, leaders, a tradition, a pride, a flag, rituals, and a set of laws. This Way of Religion becomes our extended false selves. We find our self-confidence on that nationalistic power horse. We will defend and promote it as if it were us.

If our nationalistic leaders tell us to kill people in other nations, our other horse (the Way of Wisdom) may tell us a different message. Then, we must choose to ride either our white horse or our black one.

"In no way…can a man stretch bows two." We cannot have dual intentions at the same time. For example, we cannot intend to be full of life and wisdom at the possible sacrifice of money, and at the same time, to make making money our priority over wisdom development. The first is the Way of Wisdom and the second is the Way of Religion.

"In no way, can a servant serve lords two; or, he will honor the one, and the other one, he will despise." For example: Our lord clergyperson may tell us that those who do not believe our truths live in sin. That may work fine for us for a while. However always our Way of Religion lord will get through to use and demand through soul-knowing that we identify with our core selves, not with our theology. At that point, we choose to live in darkness or light by the lord we choose to serve.

To follow Jesus and become fulfilled, we must give up the notion that we can ride two horses, pull two bows, and serve two lords. For example, we may think that we can identify with our core self AND identify with being an American, a Buddhist, a plumber, a conservative, and a male. When we do try to do that, we spend most of our time in emotional turmoil on the Way of Religion.

Jesus is clear: To be single, one identifies with one horse, one bow, and one lord all arising out of one's core inner life with our Father and Mother. One cannot do that and at the same time identify with any group of common beliefs, any symbol of such a group such as a crucifix or flag, any titles used, such as "Father," "Sister," "Mullah," or "Reverend," or any garments that shout, "I am special, you are not." As soon as one does that, he tries to ride two horses, pull two bows and serve two lords. He will be emotionally torn.

As people grow in wisdom and life, they may begin by jumping from one horse to the other, from between a Way of Religion supportive large group of family and friends to a tiny Way of Wisdom support group. Both provide an enjoyable life; however, the nature of that life is shockingly different if one has a third eye to see it. Eventually, to find peace, Jesus says one must ride one horse, pull one bow, and follow one lord.

Ways of Wisdom and Religion

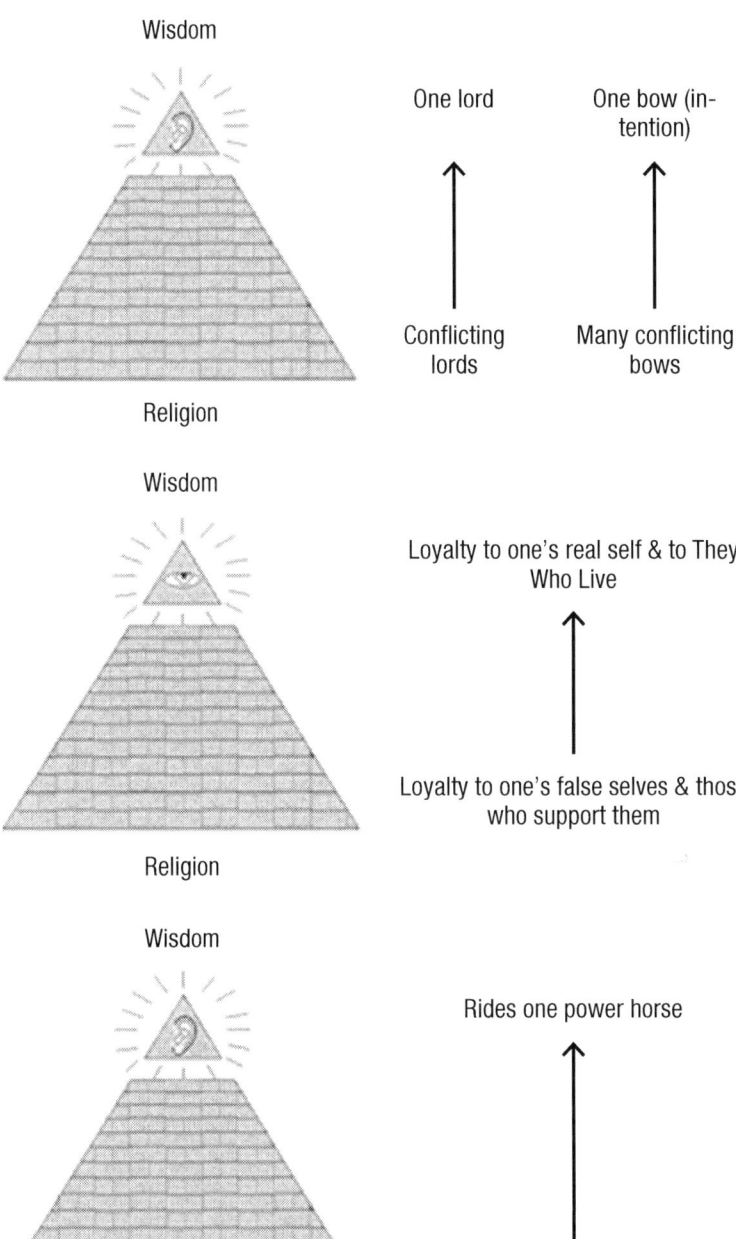

LoveGuard Indoctrinators

Jesus saw that most indoctrinators were the enemy. He tells us to love them and guard against them. Let us read the clever way he expresses this in Chapter Two, Poem Two (Saying 3a):

> Jesus
> said this:
>
> *If*
> *they*
> *should say to you*
> *this:*
>
> *Namely*
> *those,*
>
> *Who*
> *lead themselves*
> *before you:*[1,2]

[1] *Who lead themselves before you*: Clerics, politicians, parents, peers, authors and other leaders who ordain themselves to indoctrinate others with their truths.

[2] *Before you*: When Jesus uses the phrase "before you," he intends that his audience remember the many biblical commands warning us not to put false gods before us (Exodus 20:3, Exodus 32:1, 5, 2; Deuteronomy 5:7; 12:30; Judges 2:3). There are two kinds of leaders: Those that empower people to find their own answers on their own about who they are, who others are, and how the world works; and those who try to control people's thinking. The former lead on the Way of Wisdom, the latter on the Way of religion. Jesus says that when we permit leaders and peers to "lead themselves before us," we worship them as false gods.

"Behold!

*The kingdom³
is in heaven;"⁴*

*Then
the birds
of heaven⁵,⁶
will come to be
first
before you.⁷*

³*Kingdom*: A kingdom is one's high, wise rule over oneself and one's interactions with others.

⁵*Heaven*: A level of knowing.

⁴*The kingdom is in heaven*: Your rule will be found in the indoctrinator's level of believing about all. The indoctrinator says: "Believe as I do and you will be fulfilled."

⁶*Birds*: Mental ideas, most often, blind beliefs.

⁷*The birds of heaven*: the artificial beliefs of a level of knowing. When a leader says, "Your kingdom of heaven will be found in my ideas," he means, "Your way of being fulfilled as a ruler will be found in my mental, absolutely true beliefs."

⁸*Then, the birds of heaven will come to be before you*: Then, the indoctrinator's beliefs will become your false gods.

If
they
should say to you
this:

Namely   [8]*Sea*: Unconscious
those,   and semi-conscious
           emotions.

Who   [9]*The kingdom is in the*
lead themselves   *sea*: "Your rule is in
before you: true emotions." In other
           words, the indoctrinating
           leader tries to convince
"Behold!   his followers that they
           will rule when they adopt
           his emotional beliefs.

The kingdom
is   [10]*Fish*: Emotional ideas,
in the sea;"[8,9]   most often, emotional
           blind beliefs.

Then   [11]*Then the fish will come*
the fish[10]   *to be first before you*:
will come to be   Then the indoctrinating
first   leader's emotional ideas
           will come to be your false
before you.[11]   gods.

In that Poem, Jesus points out two means through which leaders indoctrinate. The first means is through logical mental arguments. He calls them, "birds," because they flit around in our brain with no basis in observable fact.

For example, an indoctrinator may show logically that Jesus is the second person in the Trinity. Based on that, the indoctrinator may then tell the audience that they need to follow the doctrine of the church that he represents. For some cerebral people, the juxtaposing of those two abstract arguments convinces them to put the indoctrinator, his church and its doctrine before them as false gods.

The second means is through emotional, sometimes illogical arguments. For example, an emotional preacher may shout, "Jesus lives, he has been resurrected." If one were to think logically, one might ask, "Does Jesus live after death any differently than anyone else?" In other words, the fact that Jesus lives and that he is resurrected does not seem to logically mean anything. Yet, the emotion of the indoctrinator moves the audience.

An emotional indoctrinator does not count on people to listen to him logically. He wants to move them emotionally to live blindly his truths at his level of heaven.

Indoctrinators create Ways of Religion by intellectually or emotionally preaching fixed, artificial truths, truths not tied to anything you can observe and validate.

People find their self-confidence in certainty; thus, they seek false-god people and institutions who will give them that, even if it means embracing artificial, illogical blind beliefs.

Jesus never knew an absolute truth. At each level of life and wisdom, he perceived the world differently. He did not seek blind-belief certainty, he trusted in the evolution of truth as it was shown him by his Parents. Each instant he gave up what he had discovered to discover more. He was a perpetual seeker and finder.

Jesus knew that for a person to be an independent ruler of his kingdom, he needed to get free of self-absorbed indoctrinators and find the unique answers given him moment to moment by his Parents. So as part of his teaching, Jesus needed to confront the enemy—all of those leaders who wished to enslave people to their low level ideas. He did that strongly in several poems, including Poem One in Chapter 10 (Saying 39):

Jesus said this:

*The Pharisees
and
the Scribes[1]
took the keys[2]
of knowledge,[3]*

*And
they
hid them,[4]*

*Nor
did
they
go inward;[5]*

And those

*Who
desired to go
inward,*

*They
did
not permit them.[6]*

[1] *Pharisees and Scribes*: Two of the many groups of clerics within Judaism. In this Gospel, they represent all indoctrinating leaders, whether religious or secular. Such leaders could be politicians, clerics, professors, parents, business managers, TV celebrities and influential friends.

[2] *Keys*: The keys to knowledge are what Jesus teaches, beginning with soul-knowing.

[3] *Knowledge*: Knowledge of your real self, the real self of others, and the principles of coming alive in a dead world.

[4] *Hid them*: Taught people to make the beliefs of authorities more important than what they soul-know.

[5] *Go inward*: Leave their indoctrination and soul-know.

[6] *They did not permit them*: The authorities taught people to distrust soul-knowing.

"And those who desired to go inward, they did not permit them." The indoctrinators insured that people became conformists by ridiculing mistakes, telling them that they were bad if they thought or acted contrary to doctrine and by marginalizing and persecuting rebels psychologically and physically.

For example, a clergy person may tell people that if they disobey the church's interpretation of scripture, they will go to hell. Or a commentator may manipulate people into thinking that if they disagree with the political party, they will be fools. Or a peer group may ostracize a member for unorthodox thinking and behavior. Or a parent may weep trying to cause emotional pain in her child who does not honor the family traditions.

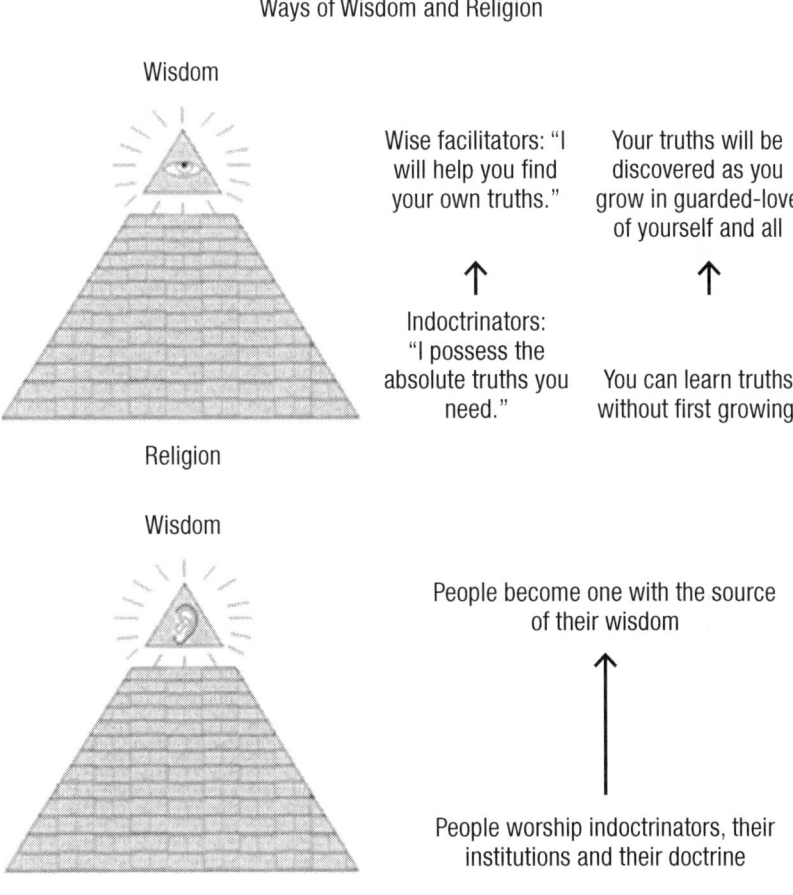

Ways of Wisdom and Religion

In contrast to people who want to be masters over others, Jesus ensured that no one relates to him like that. Let us notice how he love-guards a disciple who wants to adore him as a false-god leader in Chapter Two, Poem Three (Saying 13):

Jesus
asked his disciples:

"Compare me,

And
you
speak to me
this:

I
resemble
whom?"

Said
he
to him,

Namely
Simon Peter,
this:

"You
resemble
an angel,[1]

One,

Who
is
righteous.[2]

[1] *You resemble an angel*: You resemble someone who uses soul-knowing to communicate with God; and then, who provides that information to us.

[2] *Who is righteous*: Who lives by the laws of God.

Said
he
to him,

Namely
Matthew
this:

"You
resemble
a philosopher,[3]

One

Who
is
wise."[4]

Said
he
to him,

Namely
Thomas
this:

"Master,[5]

My entire mouth[6]
permits me
not to say:[7]

[3] *You resemble a philosopher*: You resemble someone who seeks to know himself, others, and the principles of personal development.

[4] *Wise*: Evolved.

[5] *Master*: One who controls how another thinks and acts.

[6] *Mouth*: My entire being. When one speaks from his mouth, he speaks from his being. If he identifies with his real self, he speaks from He Who Lives. If he identifies with his false self, he speaks from indoctrinators.

[7] *My entire mouth permits me not to say*: My entire being permits me not to say.

*Whom
you
resemble."*

*Jesus
said to Thomas:*

*"I
am
your master
not."*[8]

[8] *I am your master not*: Fool, become your own master in the kingdom.

"You resemble an angel." In the Old Testament, angels delivered messages from God, usually to prophets. For example, in 1Kings 13:18 we read. "I also am a prophet as you are, and an angel spoke to me by the word of the LORD."

The angels were symbols, both of a person who used soul-knowing to communicate directly with his source of inspiration, and of the message.

As one grows on the Way of Wisdom, one uses soul-knowing more; thus, one receives direct revelation and becomes an angel to others. Jesus; thus, had no problem with Peter calling him an angel. He also wanted everyone to become an angel.

"You resemble a philosopher." Everyone on the Way of Wisdom uses soul-knowing and logic to understand himself, others and the principles governing the world. Thus, again, Jesus embraced Matthew's description of him.

"Master." When Thomas called Jesus, "Master," Jesus attacked in love when he said, "I am not our master."

On the Way of Religion, people identify with titles, roles, offices, uniforms, and awards—anything to give them status over another. From that position, they believe that they have the right to be master over how others think and act.

Jesus will not endorse that abuse; consequently, he replied, **"I am not your master."** In other words, "Grow up and use soul-knowing to discover yourself on your own."

Thomas wanted an enslaving indoctrinator. Jesus empowered him to be free.

Ways of Wisdom and Religion

Wisdom

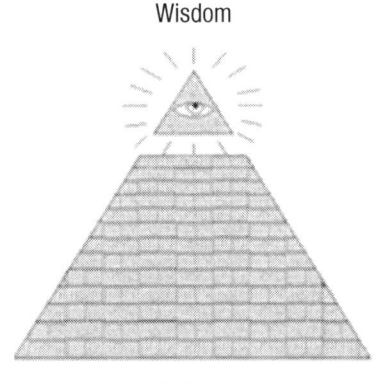

People seek facilitators, not masters.

People seek masters who use external symbols of power and specialness to dominate their thinking and behavior.

Religion

MASTER YOUR FIELDS

When we were little children we were one with our core selves. Indoctrinators taught us through the socialization process to identify with false selves and to dislike and hate those who were not like our false selves. Jesus illustrates what we must do to reverse that process on the Way of Wisdom in Poem Two, Chapter Six (Saying 21a):

Mary said to Jesus:	[1]*Disciples*: People who follow Jesus' Way of Wisdom.
"Your disciples,[1]	
They resemble whom?"[2]	[2]*They resemble whom*: They resemble whom in the way they think and act?

Jesus responded:

"*They resemble small children,*

They dwelling in a field[3]

[3]*They dwelling in a field*: A field is a person's sphere of influence. It is the internal and external environment affected by a person's presence. A field is one's sense of self, and it is a family, work environment, or group in which one finds himself.

We are more than isolated beings. The person we are affects others over a distance. For example, when a little child is brought into a room, he affects everyone. His light becomes the light in the room. How powerful he is at birth. That self he lives in and the room is his field of influence.

When a person living at a low level of heaven comes into the room, we sense the darkness. We also sense the light in others. Their fields influence us.

When a person chooses to live from a false self, he causes his real self to suffer. He affects his own field. For example, he becomes afraid, depressed, anxious and angry. In other words, he makes himself emotionally sick.

With mass communication, a person's field can be worldwide.

A little child does not know to guard; consequently, it can be seduced by someone's dark field.

Which
is
not theirs.[4]

When
they
should come,

Namely
the lords
of the field,[5]

They
will say this:

'Release our field
back to us.'[6]

And
they
will strip naked[7]
in their presence,[8]

[4] *Which is not theirs.* The followers of Jesus live at a high level of heaven. They may work and live around people on the Way of Religion at a low level. So they dwell superficially in a low level "which is not theirs."

[5] *When they should come, namely, the lords of the field*: A lord of a field is a leader. For example, a lord could be a parent at the Christmas dinner, or a boss at work, or a friend at lunch.

[6] *Release our field back to us*: Conform to our level of thinking and acting. For example at the Christmas dinner, a parent may say, "Pray like we do." Or a boss may say, "We cover for each other. No one upstairs need know." A friend may say, "Go along until you find another job."

[7] *They will strip naked*: The child-adult followers of Jesus refuse to be what they are not; thus, they easily strip themselves of false-self clothes and pay the costs.

[8] *In their presence*: To declare openly one's real self.

So that *it* *be given back* *to them."⁹*	[9]*So that it be given back to them*: So that those on a Way of Religion can have their level of knowing and deceit.
And *it* *will be given back* *to them."¹⁰*	[10]*And it will be given back to them*: So that those demanding to control a field may choke on their false identities.

"They resemble small children, they dwelling in a field, which is not theirs." Jesus describes the war of fields that we encounter every day. No two people live exactly on the same level of heaven. The greater the distance between fields, the greater the conflict.

"When they should come, namely the lords of the field, they will say this: 'Release our field back to us." Lords of the field sense when someone does not conform to falseness. Then, they have an option: To look at themselves with soul-knowing and decide if they have something to learn from the non-conformist, or remain blind and demand that the rebel meet their standards.

"And they will strip naked in their presence, so that it be given back to them."

The person on the Way of Wisdom soul-knows deliberately every other person's field. In every encounter, he chooses to strip rather than compromise or lie, to love-guard rather than be controlled. He will lose a job or be banished from a community rather than live at a lower level.

Ways of Wisdom and Religion

Wisdom

Religion

| Clings to external symbols of power and specialness → Easily strips himself of external symbols of power and specialness | Hides who he is out of fear of the costs of being himself → Honestly discloses who he is and pays the costs |

Wisdom

Religion

Loves and guards his false-self and abandons others no matter the cost → Love-Guards his real-self and others at any cost

Wisdom

Religion

| Manifests low fields of wisdom and life → Manifests high fields of wisdom and life | Auto-Triggers approval & support from low lifers → Auto-Triggers anger and jealousy in low lifers |

Jesus' observed that we pass our fields on to our sons, daughters and neighbors in Chapter 21, Poem Three (Saying 109):

Jesus responded:

The kingdom[1] is comparable to a man,

Who had he there in his field[2] a treasure[3,4] hidden,[5]

He not knowing about it.[6]

And after he died,[7]

He left it to his son;[8] And the son did not know about it.[9]

[1] *Kingdom*: A "field." It is an internal and external area of personal rule.

[2] *Field*: Internal and external sphere of personal influence.

[3] *Treasure*: Words of wisdom that can only be soul-known.

[4] *Man..who had...treasure*: All men have in their possession a treasure of wisdom, but only those who are soul-alert know about it.

[5] *It hidden*: It concealed by his living death, by his Ways of Religion.

[6] *Not knowing about it*: People on the Way of Religion do not know that they possess the ability to disclose to themselves the wisdom about who they are, who others are, and how to solve practical problems.

[7] *After he died*: After he grew more and more to live death.

[8] *Son*: A person who learns a tradition from a father.

[9] *Son did not know about it*: The son did not know about hidden wisdom. He lived loyal to the Ways of Religion he inherited from his various fathers.

*He
took the field,

Which
was
there,*[10]

*And
he
gave it
away.*[11]

*And
whoever
bought it,*[12]

*He
came*[13]
plowing,[14]

*And
he
discovered the treasure;*[15]

*And
he
began to give money
at interest*[16]
to those,

*Whom
he
desired.*[17]

[10]*Took the field which was there*: Took the awareness that is known only by living in the present.

[11]*And gave it away*: He did not know that he has something of value.

[12]*Bought it*: Paid the price of differing from others to be on the Way of Wisdom. Paid the price of being loyal to his real self when others wanted him to conform to their false Ways.

[13]*He came*: Came into a level of awareness in the moment.

[14]*He plowing*: He examined what he soul-knew.

[15]*Discovered the treasure*: The meaning for his life of the wisdom he soul-discovered.

[16]*Give money at interest*: He spoke out of love-guardedness.
He used his words of wisdom to help others while demanding a responsible response.

[17]*Whom he desired*: Whom he desired to share his divine life. In other words, he did not speak wisdom to everyone, because he knows who is receptive and who will not use those words responsibly.

"And after he died, he died, he left it to his son." And after living on the Way of Religion until he, as a robot, thought and acted as he was indoctrinated, he taught his son to live the same Way. He could have taught his son to be rebel and discover his own answers with soul-knowing; however, he did not.

For example, when parents teach a child their fears about the future and guilt about the past, the child may rebel, or he may buy into the death world of his parents. When he choose the latter course, he grows up dead and may teach his child to live death.

"And whoever bought it, he came plowing, and he discovered the treasure." Occasionally, a person comes along, pays the price of being a non-conformist, and begins down the Way of Wisdom. He grows in soul-knowing, questions authorities, leaves blind beliefs, confronts himself, lives the pain and joys that he discovers, and continues soul-listening until he breaks through to his real life answers—his treasure.

Ways of Wisdom and Religion

Wisdom

Discovers his own treasure of wisdom and empowers others to do the same

↑

Lives the world's truths and indoctrinates others in them

Religion

Seek to Destroy Yourself

To evolve on the Way of Wisdom, one must trample what he has taken on as precious extension of himself. Jesus states that in Chapter Nine, Poem Four (Saying 37):

Jesus responded:

"When
you
should strip yourselves naked[1]
without being ashamed,[2]

And
you
take your garments[3]

And
you
put them
on the earth[4]
under your feet[5]

Like
those little,
small children [6]
do,

[1] *When you strip yourselves naked*: When you stop presenting yourself as anything but your core, light self. Or when you stop identifying yourself with ideas, things and people.

[2] *Without being ashamed*: Without worrying about whether you conform to the expectations of others.

[3] *Garments*: Those beliefs, things and people to which you identify rather than your core life.

[4] *Earth*: Our reflective consciousness. To put garments on the earth is to bring into consciousness one's false identifications and the harm they cause to oneself and others.

[5] *Feet*: What we stand on for confidence. When we take a stand in the world, we project ourselves from the beliefs, things and people important to us.

[6] *Little, small children*: People who love themselves for being who they are, not what they are with clothes (false identities) on.

And you trample them;⁷	⁷*Trample them*: See those clothes (false identities) as foolish and useless. To trample is to demean what gave one false life.
Then you will peer upon the son of He Who lives,⁸	⁸*Son of He Who Lives*: Then, you will reveal yourself and the core of another as the son or daughter of They Who Live.
And you will come to be afraid not.⁹	⁹*Come to be afraid not*: Come to be emotionally healthy.

"And you take your garments." And you identify your false identities. For example, you look at your appearance and how proud it makes you. Or you see how hard you have worked to have a title and a position that makes you appear important for the wrong reasons.

"And you put them on the earth under your feet." And you deliberately stand on them to see how awful they feel to yourself and others. For example, you recognize how flaunting your appearance has made yourself look silly and others feel inferior. Or you recall how you have used your title and position to control others, rather than free them to find their own answers.

"And you trample them." And you make them nothing to you. For example, you see how worthless your false identities are compared to being who you are honestly in the world, no matter the cost.

"And you will become afraid not:" To the degree that one identifies with beliefs, things, and people, to that degree he lives in fear of losing them. For example, If one stands on money, he fears loss. If one stands on his beliefs, he fears being shown he is wrong. If one stands on his spouse, he fears losing her.

Fear may be the basis of all emotional problems. When we grieve, we fear the consequences of a past loss. When we get frustrated, we fear failure. When we become out-of-body excited, we fear being still with our painful emotions.

Jesus tells us that we stop being fearful when we trample our identification with ideas, people and things. A woman afraid of losing her spouse must trample her dependency and claim herself standing alone. A child afraid to fail must trample his shame and claim his dignity with doing his best. The permissive mother who is afraid of losing her children must trample her obsession with giving them all that they want and claim how wonderful she is whether her children like or not. A man who is afraid to say to his child, "I love you," must trample his false manliness and claim his tenderness.

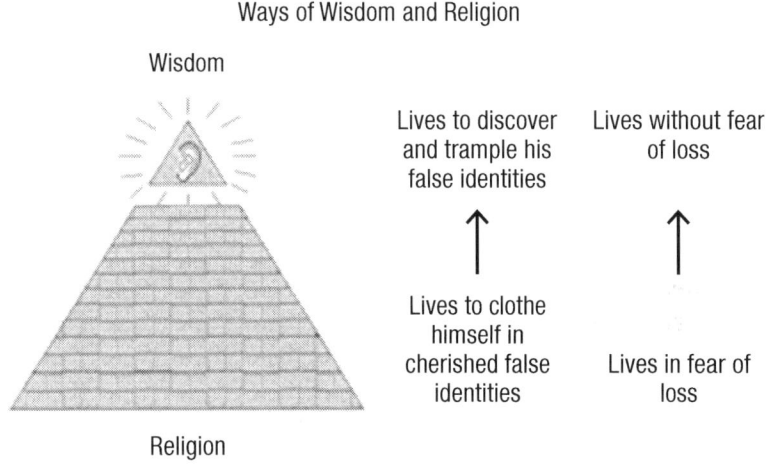

Destroy Your Divided Self

We know from the following Poem that Jesus was not born perfect. He identified with false selves thanks to his socialization by his birth mother. When very young, he entered the war of fields with his mother and those around him who wanted him to conform to Judaism, his Jewish tradition, and to do the things that would be safe in a Roman dominated country. He also went to war with himself. He was generating two fields, by riding two horses, pulling two bows, and serving two lords. His false-selves wanted approval and support from those around him. His real-self wanted to be more alive no matter the cost. Over and over again, he decided to destroy his false selves as he says in Chapter 16, Poem Four (Saying 71):

Jesus said this:

I will destroy this house [1,2]

And no one can build it,[3]

Never.

[1] *House*: A self. Our house has rooms when it has false selves. When it is empty, we are our real self.

[2] *I will destroy this house*: I will destroy this house with rooms (false identities).

[3] *And No one can build it*: And no one can manipulate me into identifying with false selves again. No one can convince me to stand on religious beliefs, family traditions, money, political beliefs, things and people. I will stand on my core, divine, real self.

Ways of Wisdom and Religion

Wisdom

Destroys rooms in his house

Love-Guards himself from house dividers

↑

↑

Builds rooms in his house

Loves house dividers

Religion

Having destroyed his house with false rooms over and over, Jesus was able to formulate a universal Way of Wisdom principle for self-development in Chapter 13, Poem Two (Saying 61):

Jesus
said this:

"When
he
should come to be
destroyed,[1]

He
will be
full
of light.[2]

When
however,

He
should come to be
divided,[3]

He
will be
full
of darkness.[4]

[1] *Come to be destroyed*: When he stops identifying with his false selves. When he stops identifying with any set of theological or secular beliefs.

[2] *Light*: The power emanating from honesty.

[3] *Divided*: Divided in loyalty between his real self and his false selves.

[4] *Darkness*: Dishonesty, confusion, and fear.

"Light…Darkness:" Emotionally sound…emotionally ill. We often see emotional illness as normal. Jesus did not.

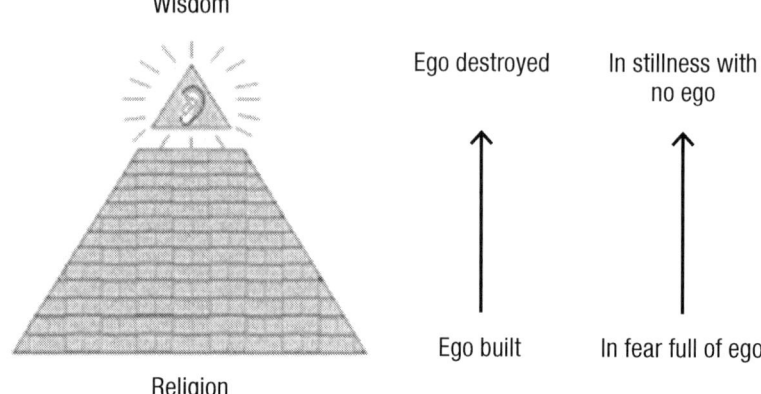

Get Lost

Jesus provides a model of a great leader who seeks out those lost on the Way of Wisdom in Chapter 20, Poem Seven (Saying 107):

The kingdom, [1]	[1] *Kingdom*: A realm or field of influence ruled by an egoless king or queen.
It is comparable to a man shepherding, [2]	[2] *Man shepherding*: A man who loves and guards all.
Who had he there 100 sheep. [3]	[3] *Sheep*: People.
One of them strayed, [4]	[4] *Strayed*: Became a nonconformist.
The greatest was he.[5]	[5] *The greatest was he*: He became great because he began to soul-know himself and others on his own.

Jesus' Self-Development Method

He let go the 99,[6] *And he sought after that one*[7] *Until he discovered it troubled.*[8]	[6]*99*: Those on the Way of Religion. [7]*One*: Rebel. [8]*Troubled*: Troubled because he knew deep down that he was divided, but he could not find the Way of Wisdom to singleness. People conform to group-think in order to avoid emotional trouble.

"And he sought after that one until he found it troubled." People conform to group-think in order to avoid emotional trouble. A non-conformist seeks himself and always finds at first, trouble. Thus, a seeker seeks to stray, to be lost, to be "troubled," and to be found by a wise shepherd. He suffers that quest daily.

The shepherd may be another person or what he senses directly from his Parents in soul-knowing. If it is another person, he soul-listens to him in love-guardedness to be sure that he protects himself from false messages.

Ways of Wisdom and Religion

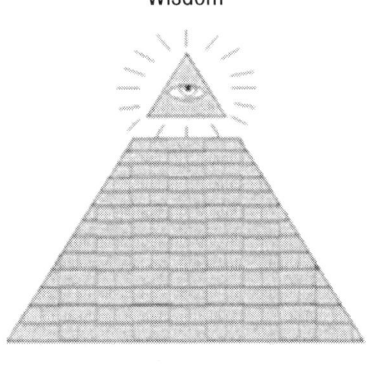

Wisdom

Rebels seeking emotional trouble in order to be found by wise shepherds

Conformists seeking emotional comfort from false shepherds

Religion

Become in the Beginning

Whenever we face any problem, we become emotionally upset, which is a sign that we are living in the past, future or in both. When we live in the present, we are never upset. We are movement from stillness.

So whenever we are upset, we know we are on the Way of Religion, that is, we know that we have identified with our clothes (false identities).

Those who have decided to live on the Way of Wisdom therefore seek a shepherd to lead them back to living in the moment. Jesus says that in Poem One from Chapter Five (Saying 18a):

The disciples said to Jesus:	[1]*End*: The disciples could have been asking about their personal end after following Jesus. The disciples could have been asking about the end of Jesus's mission. They could have been asking about the end of times. In all three of those questions, they seek their end in the future.
"Speak to us this:	
Our end[1] will come to be in what manner?"	
Jesus responded:	
"Have you revealed yourself in the beginning,[2]	[2]*Have you revealed yourself in the beginning*: Have you revealed your true self in the present?
So that you will be seeking after the end?[3]	[3]*Have you revealed yourself in the beginning; so that you will be seeking after the end*: Have you become you before you begin to proceed; so that you know and are your goal?
For in the place[4]	[4]*Place*: That part of us within from which we think and act.

Where the beginning is there,[5]	[5]*Where the beginning is there*: Where stillness in the now begins to reside.
The end will come to be there."[5]	[5]*For in the place where the beginning is there, the end will come to be there*: For how you begin the journey to a fulfilled life is how you will end it.

"OUR END WILL COME IN WHAT MANNER?"

The word "end" may have been one of the most thought-about and used concepts in the 1st century Jewish world. The people of Palestine were being literally taxed to death by Herod and the Romans. The people longed for the dignity and freedom that their ancestors had when David ruled in about 800 BCE. They saw the greed, dishonesty and general lack of living the Torah in their religious leaders. They longed for a cleansed temple leadership that would inspire people and not exploit them. And so they longed for the end to their physical and psychological/spiritual suffering.

The end of this age of darkness and the beginning of a new age of light was greatly anticipated because of the predictions of key Jewish prophets. For example in Daniel 8:17-19 we read:

> *So he came near where I stood; and when he came, I was frightened and fell upon my face. But he said to me, "Understand, O son of man, that the vision is for the time of the end." As he was speaking to me, I fell into a deep sleep with my face to the ground; but he touched me and set me on my feet. He said, "Behold, I will make known to you what shall be at the latter end of the indignation; for it pertains to the appointed time of the end.*

In the above passage, "son of man" refers to the coming Messiah.

About that Messiah, Malachi predicted (Mal 3:2):

> *But who can endure the day of his coming, and who can stand when he appears? "For he (no") is like a refiner's fire and like fullers' soap.*

So the people expected that the Messiah will preach such a strong message, and be such a strong person that one will wonder who can stand in his presence. His message will burn those who are duplicitous, and cleanse those who wish to live a pure life.

Ezra proclaimed the most moving predictions of the coming of the Messiah at the end of this age of corruption.

> *Therefore I say to you, O nations that hear and understand, "Await your shepherd; he will give you everlasting rest, because he who will come at the end of the age is close at hand. (4 Ezra 2:34). But the day of judgment will be the end of this age and the beginning of the immortal age to come, in which corruption has passed away (4 Ezra 7:113)."*

It is also Ezra that spoke specifically about the Messiah who would be of the lineage of David and how he would first judge the wicked and second, free the innocent (4 Ezra 12:32-34).

> *The Messiah whom the Most High has kept until the end of days, who will arise from the posterity of David, and will come and speak to them; he will denounce them for their ungodliness and for their wickedness, and will cast up before them their contemptuous dealings. For first he will set them living before his judgment seat, and when he has reproved them, then he will destroy them. But he will deliver in mercy the remnant of my people, those who have been saved throughout my*

> *borders, and he will make them joyful until the end comes, the day of judgment, of which I spoke to you at the beginning*

Those are but a few of the many predictions that Jesus' disciples had memorized. Thus when they asked Jesus about the end, we know that it resonated with many deep, powerful personal and community longings:

> "Speak to us
> this:
> *Our end
> will come to be
> in what manner?"*

The disciples hoped that Jesus was the Messiah; however, they may not have seen in him what they expected. So in disappointment, they asked him vaguely as a prophet, and not the Messiah, to "tell us how our end will come about."

"Have you revealed yourself in the beginning, so that you will be seeking after the end?"

Jesus did not buy in to their false dream that they would be different when the Messiah arrived. He pointed to their responsibility to be in the beginning. He knew that this is THE task, the most difficult task for a person on his Way. He knew that when they were in the present moment, they would know their end, and know how to seek it in each moment.

"For in the place where the beginning is there, the end will come to be there." For when you change that place from where you live to movement from stillness, you will become the end and the Messiah for yourself and others.

Jesus does not say that there will not be a Messiah; rather he makes that person subordinate to what a person can become on his own. He rephrases Ezra 9:5

> *For just as with everything that has occurred in the world, the beginning is evident, and the end manifest.*

Jesus knows that all worry, regret, false-excitement, depression, sadness, fear, longing—all emotional issues will be resolved only when one becomes oneself in the "beginning," that is, in the present. Once a person knows who he is, his core seeking is over. He proceeds in movement from joyful stillness to solve any secondary problem.

If we begin in movement from regret, worry and/or out-of-self excitement every idea we obtain will lead to more regret, worry and/or out-of-self excitement, so we learn not to begin like this. We may think or do something that covers up our beginning regret and worry and/or out-of-self excitement; however, our problems have not been resolved. Therefore, they will come back to destroy us.

If we begin in movement from joyful stillness, every idea we obtain will lead always to more. We cannot get there from here if here is different from there. If "here" is misery, "there" will be also. If "here" is movement from stillness in the beginning, "there" will be also.

Thus, his core message in that poem to all of us: Stop dreaming about someone else saving you, you become the savior of yourself and the world by revealing yourself in the beginning.

When we are in emotional pain, our Way of Wisdom indoctrination tells us to seek relief in the future. We pray for future relief, we go into the future to buy and read books, to meet with friends to discuss our problems, to distract ourselves

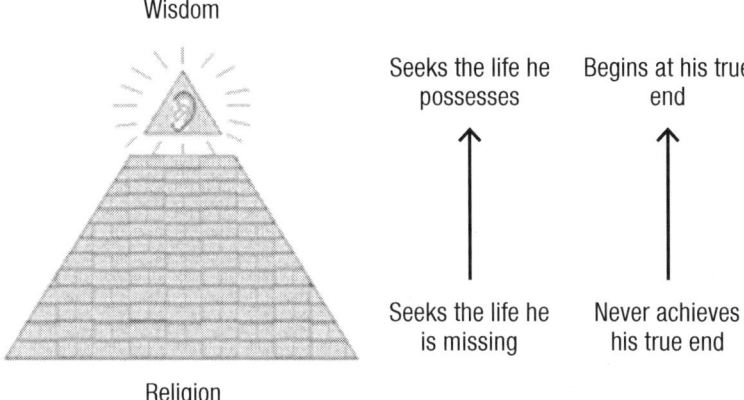

by buying things, or by losing ourselves in activities such as sex, music, art, and gambling. We have endless ways of seeking our real, still selves in the future. When we do that we are like the disciples who sought the end of one age of misery and the beginning of an age of fulfillment.

Everything the Way of Religion has taught must be reversed or thrown out—everything. We cannot ride two horses, pull two bows or serve two lords.

When we are miserable, we might yank ourselves out of the Way of Religion by reciting to ourselves the following Poem Three from Chapter Five (Saying 19a):

"A blessed one is he who will come to be from the beginning before he comes to be." A blessed one is he who will come to be love-guarded of all before proceeding.

A blessed one[1]
is
he,

Who
will come to be[2]
from the beginning,[3]

Before
he
comes to be.[4]

[1] *A blessed one*: A wise one.

[2] *Will come to be*: Will come to be fully alive in love-guarded of all.

[3] *From the beginning*: From this moment.

[4] *Before he comes to be*: Before he seeks to be involved in the solution of any other problem.

When we are afraid (upset), we dislike what is happening now, what happened in the past, or what might happen in the future. Dislike is mild hate. In other words, all upset arises from fear and hate.

All solutions arise when we are love-guarded from stillness. To be still in the beginning, we need to love-guard what is going on. Recall Poem Five from Chapter Eight (Saying 25)

Love your brother

Like
your soul.

Guard him

Like
the pupil
of your eye.

"Love your brother like your soul." Love all that has life like your core soul; in other words, love all.

"All" includes all of our mistakes, all of our enemies, all that our enemies did to us, all of our health issues…all the darkness that surrounds us.

To evolve, we must decide which horse we will ride and which bow we will pull: The light horse and the bow of love, or the black horse and the bow of hate. One horse rides into self-destruction of our ego (false selves) and freedom, the other into enhancement of our ego and enslavement, one into living in the past and future, the other to being oneself in the beginning.

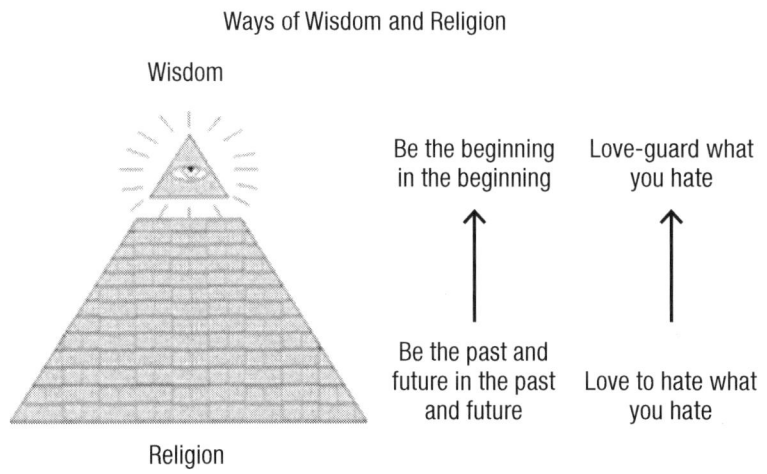

Jesus shows us that by being in the beginning, we attack. In other words, the best defense, is a great offence. He says that and more in Chapter Six, Poem Five (Saying 21):

Jesus
said this:

*You
therefore,*

*Keep watch
from the beginning
of the world,* [1,2,3]

Bind yourselves[4]
in a great power;[5]

*So that
not
the thieves*[6]
discover the entrance[7]
to the way[8]
*to come up
to you.*[9]

*Because,
the help,*[10]

[1] *World*: One's world one creates whenever one chooses either the Way of Wisdom or the Way of Religion.

[2] *Beginning of the world*: Each moment is the beginning of one's world.

[3] *Keep watch from the beginning of the world*: Stop drifting, be conscious each moment of your opportunity to be present with what is going on.

[4] *Bind yourselves*: Bind your loins. Pull yourself together with conviction.

[5] *Great power*: A strong sense of your core divine life. Be love-guarded.

[6] *Thieves*: Those on the Way of Religion including your lower self.

[7] *Discover the entrance*: Discover your weaknesses.

[8] *Way*: The Way of Wisdom.

[9] *To come up to you*: To seduce you.

[10] *Help*: Insights.

For which *you* *peer outward,*[11] *It* *is* *that,* *Which* *will be discovered* *in yourselves.*[12]	[11]*The help for which you peer outward*: For that which you seek from the Messiah and from dead people and their authorities, such as therapists, clergy, authors, friends, etc. on the Way of Religion. [12]*It is that which will be discovered in yourselves*: It is that which will be discovered with soul-knowing in oneness with They Who Live.

"Keep watch from the beginning of the world." Do not wander through your day and allow yourself to be manipulated into doing some will of a false lord.

"Bind yourselves in a great power." Bring yourself together in love-guarded of all, no matter what happens.

"To love" all is to experience all as perfect, just the way it is. We fully embrace the worst that has or will happen, from torture to finding out that a loved one has terminal cancer, to the death of our physical bodies.

To guard all is to see the true limitations of all. Nothing is perfect in the sense of being without limitation or fault.

To love/guard all is not to approve all or condemn all. Rather, it is to be love as we face, accept, respect, and sometimes, improve all.

"So that not the thieves discover the entrance to the way to come up to you." Our thieves are ourselves ultimately. We leave ourselves vulnerable to surprises. To be alert, one must love-guard the present. The love reveals the essence of everyone and every event. The guarding protects us. Love-guarding is an attitude that the wise foster.

When we wishy-washy love, we go into a dream about others. When we keep our guard up and do not love, we never see, less enjoy the true nature of others. We love-guard or die.

"For which you peer outward." When unwise, we seek salvation outward in others, such as the perfect mate or friend, the perfect advice, and the all-knowing leader.

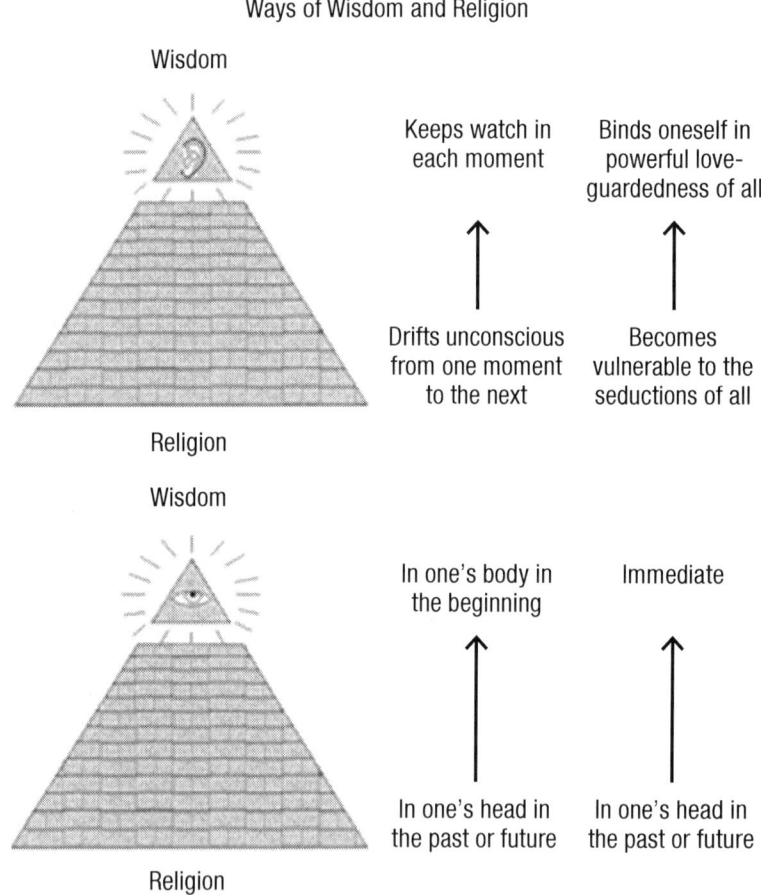

"It is that which will be discovered in yourselves." Ultimately we need do discover our own answers through soul-knowing, even if the stimulus comes from something someone else says.

In the Gospel of Thomas, Jesus gives many examples of people succumbing to thieves breaking into their kingdoms. For example, let us watch a man mirror us as he struggles to be in the beginning in Chapter 14, Poem One (Saying 63a):

Jesus said this:

There was a man of wealth[1]

Who had he there,[2]

Many riches.[3]

Said he this:

"I will make use of my riches by sowing and reaping, and planting,[4] and filling my treasure-house[5] with fruit;[6]

So that I will not need anything."[7]

[1] *Man of wealth*: The man possessed in his core-self everything that he needed, especially the divine intelligence that would lead him to more fulfillment.

[2] *There*: In the beginning.

[3] *Many riches*: He is rich with soul-knowing and with They Who Live within him.

[4] *Sowing, reaping and planting*: Sowing and reaping, then, planting and reaping, over and over again.

[5] *And filling my treasure-house*: And filling the core of my being.

[6] *Fruit*: Fulfillment.

[7] *So that I will not need anything*: So that I will not worry about needing anything in the future.

These
were his thoughts

That
were
in his heart;[8]

And
in the night[9]

Which
was
there,[10]

He
died.[11]

[8]*These were the thoughts that were in his heart*: The pivotal thoughts: "Will work for the future so that I will not need anything." In other words: "I am not going to seek myself in the beginning, rather, I am going to seek the money, things, beliefs and people that will ensure that I have a fulfilled self in the future," and then, be in the beginning.
These were the thoughts he loved most deeply. He did not love most being himself in the now.

[9]*And in the night*: As soon as he created worry and longing, it became a dark "night" for him.

[10]*Which was there*: Which was in the beginning.

[11]*He died*: He did not physically die. He stopped being alive alive, and started living a false self that stood on beliefs, money, things, and the people that he foolishly thought would bring him what he most deeply wanted in the future.

"So that I will not need anything." When we are not ourselves in the beginning, we need everything. When we are ourselves in the beginning, we need nothing.

The man was empty. He thought he needed money, beliefs, things, and friends to become full. Wanting things or having things is not bad; rather, when we want those fruits more than the fruits that come with being ourselves in the present, we get emotionally sick. In other words, when we fear not having enough, and when we regret all the things we could have done to get more, we choose fear, regret, and false enthusiasm. In that way we die in the "night."

Remember that Jesus discovered that life has its own intelligence. It moves of its own hand. It knows all. It knows that we need food, friends and other things. When we live the light, which we

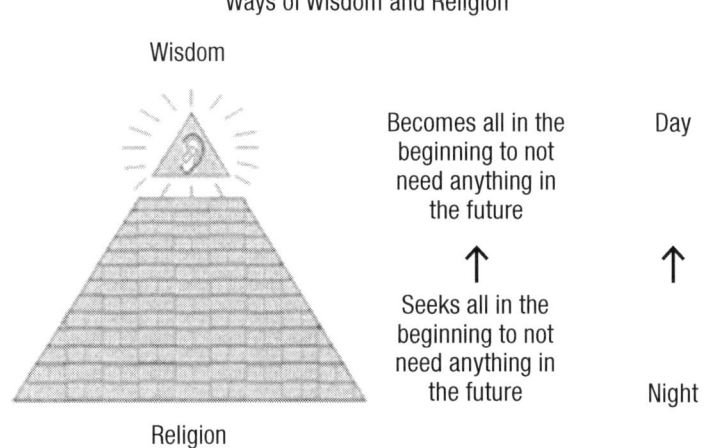

can only do in the beginning, we are led through soul-knowing to obtain what we need. When we leave our beginning to worry about getting things in the future, we may get them; however they will be accompanied by greater regret, worry and false excitement.

Jesus indicates that when we become in the beginning, and then, we let ourselves be guided to what we most deeply and unconsciously need, we will be lead to very different things and people, and a very different life. If we choose to be in the beginning, it will lead us to another beginning. If we choose to be in the future, it will lead us to another unsatisfying future—until we learn that what we want is in the beginning. To prove his point, we only need to reflect on our experience.

So Jesus noticed that our thieves (inner and outer worried voices) tell us that we may not get what we may need in the future, and that we may suffer and even die. So the choice is ours: Be in the beginning and know that even if we physically die, we will never die; or be in the future, and die now, in the next moment, and the next, until we choke on our physical death. Or to put it another way, we can love our current situation, guard ourselves from its limitations, and then, seek to change it; or we can hate our situation while seeking a better situation in the future. The former is Jesus' Way, the latter is the way of the world.

We are governed by our present beliefs. If we believe that it all happens by chance, we will forever live death worry. Jesus implies in so many poems that if we suspend our indoctrinated beliefs and look at the evidence that intelligent light has always brought us to the perfect opportunity to evolve, we will see that life is coordinated behind what we see as luck and chance. We must prove to ourselves that we become still and fulfilled when we choose to embrace what we have as perfect, just how it is. The proof is in the pudding, not in the world's blind beliefs.

His summary of his secret for a fulfilled life is in Poem Two (Saying 18a) in Chapter Five:

| Jesus said this:

A blest one
is
he

Who
will stand on his feet[1]
in the beginning

And
he
will know the end,[2]
And
he
will take a taste
not
of death."[3] | [1]*Stand on his feet*: To be strong, firm and present in the world. To possess all-confidence, because you are one with all.

[2]*And he will know the end*: The divine intelligence that is one with his real self will show him the next step that he can take to accomplish a goal while remaining in the present.

[3]*He will take a taste not of death*: He will not be frustrated, angry, anxious, depressed, grieving, jealous, and full of longing for things in the future. |

"A blest one is he who will stand on his feet in the beginning." A wise one is he who becomes all-confident by standing on the light that he is in the beginning. A stupid one is he who becomes self-confident by standing on a person, a family,

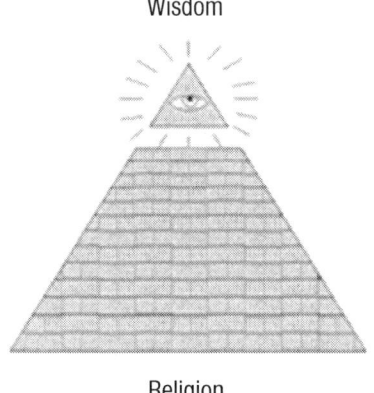

Ways of Wisdom and Religion

Wisdom

Destroys self-confidence to be all-confident
(confident in the life in all)

Seeks to be self-confident (confident in one's superior or strong traits, things and relationships)

Religion

a job, a reputation, money, appearance, a nation, a tradition, indoctrinators, and other people and things—that he could lose and that will never yield movement from stillness.

"And he will take a taste not of death." Even if he physically dies. Recall that from a high level of soul-knowing Jesus saw the evidence that:

We
have come outward
of the light,

The place,

Where
the light
comes to be
there,

Outward
by its own hand.

Now, he leaves it up to us to validate his observation that we are eternal light no matter what happens.

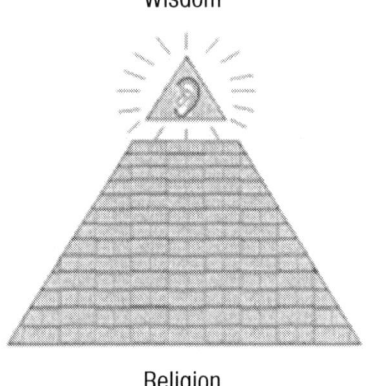

Ways of Wisdom and Religion

SEEK AND FIND

Jesus has set a lot of goals, such as:

- Be oneself,

- Be love-guarded, and

- Be in the beginning before coming to be.

He also spells out a five-step process to achieve all of the Way of Wisdom goals in the following from Chapter Two, Poem Two (Saying 2):

Jesus said this:

Let not him stop,¹

Namely he,

Who seeks,²

As he seeks,³

Until he finds.⁴

when he should find,⁵

He will be troubled.⁶

And if he should be troubled,⁷

¹*Let not him stop*: Let not him stop seeking a higher heaven of life and wisdom.

²*He who seeks*: He who seeks to evolve.

³*He who seeks as he seeks*: He who soul-seeks behind his soul-seeking. Now that is seeking!

⁴*Finds*: What he most deeply wants. For example, our minds may want a million dollars yesterday; while our souls want us to be fulfilled at a higher level of wisdom and life.

⁵*He should find*: An insight or vision showing him how he is living the Way of Religion and how he might begin to live the Way of Wisdom.

⁶*When he should find, he will be troubled*: When he should find his false self, how he lives for others rather than himself, how he is dishonest, how he clings to the past and yearns for the future to save him, how… and how…he will be troubled.

⁷*And if he should be troubled*: And if he works through his trouble to resolution at a higher level of self and other knowing.

He will come to marvel;[10]	[10]*He will come to marvel*: He will come to see everything in a new, wonderful way, come to be amazed that he chose death rather than life.
And marveling,	
He will come to reign[11] *over all;*	[11]*And marveling, he will come to reign*: As he wonders about this new way to be, he will see how to rule over himself and his interactions with others in a more enlightened manner. He will be more noble, more aware, more wise, more in control of his destiny.
And reigning,	
He will come to be still[12] *with all.*	[12]*And reigning, he will come to be still*: And as he implements changes, he will come to enjoy more deeply being movement from stillness.

In general, Jesus explains his five-step development process as:

1. Seek all day long until you recognized that you are no longer in the beginning.

2. Seek to know how you became troubled. Keep searching until you soul-see your way out.

3. Seek to know that you have transcended your trouble. You will know that when you marvel that you have risen above yourself to a new way to be.

4. With the new insights, soul-seek to use them to reign as a much stronger, wiser, more authoritative person; and finally,

5. Enjoy being again in the beginning at a new level of freedom and wisdom.

"Let not him stop, namely he, who seeks, as he seeks, until he finds." All day long, a seeker seeks to know if he has chosen to be in the beginning or in the past or future, that is, if he is movement from stillness, or movement from busyness

When he experiences regret, worry, or out-of-presence excitement, he knows that he is in the past and/or future, that he has chosen to not be himself, and that he is not love-guarding everything that happened and will happen. Instead he is running from hate (dislike) of something to false-love (liking) of something else.

For example, a seeker may throughout the day take a moment with his coffee to sit and ask himself, "What am I experiencing?" It will either be regret, worry, out-of-presence excitement or soul-joy. If it is soul-joy, he knows that he is movement from stillness in the beginning. If it is regret, worry, or false excitement, he knows that he has chosen to be movement from busyness, that he is mulling things from the past, or worrying about something in the future.

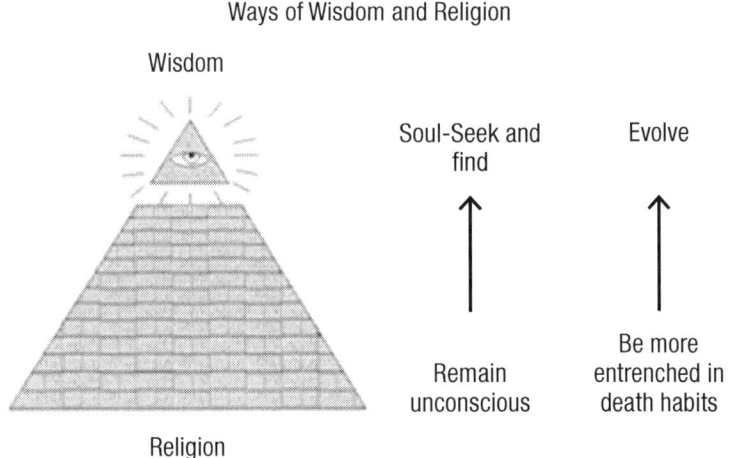

"And when he should find, he will be troubled." When a seeker finds that he is not movement from stillness, he stops everything and seeks to be troubled by the cause of his restlessness. His soul-knowing will eventually show him the false-self and beliefs

that he has chosen. It will also show him what he needs to do to evolve.

To continue the previous example, let us suppose that the person sitting with his coffee soul-discovers that he is living in past regret, or future worry or out-of-presence excitement. Now he must be troubled.

He does that by soul-asking himself, "What would I need to give up to be now in the beginning?" After some time, it may be revealed to him that he:

- Might sacrifice being late for something to be still with his coffee until he enjoys the table, the scene out the window, his body, his problems, his successes and himself, more than anything else in the past or future,

- Might sacrifice disliking someone to love-guard that person,

- Might sacrifice regretting a mistake to love-guard himself and all that happened, or

- Might sacrifice being excited to soul-recognizing that he has all now.

Ultimately, to be again in the beginning, he will need to choose to be love-guarded in the world rather than have or be anything else. In love-guardedness, one finds himself.

All of us find it difficult to understand love-guardedness. The term says everything and nothing. It is an experience unlike any other. It is the transcendent-high experience one seeks in sex, drugs, creativity and thrills.

When one love-guards, he does NOT approve of a person or an event. One embraces him or it as him or it is, rather than run from him or it. It is open-hearted being one with all.

When one guards, one recognizes the limitations and darkness in it for him. Love-guarding is not fools love, or guarding without loving either.

When a woman finds herself at an awkward moment not able to be intimate because of a flashback to a molestation event, how does she pull herself together and love-guard the perpetrator and every detail in that event? She can only do that through the power of Light that she opens to live.

When one recognizes that he has cancer and a young family, how does he love guard himself, the disease, and all that he wants to curse? He can only do that by dying to the false self that wants to be angry, sad and anxious.

When a man hears a bang and begins to tremble because what he experienced in combat stole his body-awareness that life is safe, how does he love-guard so many horrors? Only soul-knowing can show him how.

Ultimately, we all have PTSD in some form. A child body-knows that he is safe; thus, he does not have PTSD. As we live, we get brainwashed into believing that bad luck happens, or a good God causes bad things to happen, or that life isn't fair, or some other ultimately terrifying nonsense. Then, we find evidence that those beliefs are true. And then, if we live through a truly horrific event, we body-lose all sense of being safe.

The only way out is to evolve on Jesus' Way of Wisdom. We must re-experience all that haunts us, all that we project will haunt us, and become in the beginning with those people and events in love-guardedness. Gradually, we will know that nothing truly dies, and that we are safe.

For example, a person who has a flash back to an IED that killed his buddy and maimed him must immediately become one with something real to ground him, such as a child or the smile of a friend. As he opens to become one with the life in the child and friend, his body begins to open to see that the IED event was also full of perfect life. As he continues to open and be one with real life, he will also body-realize that death is impossible. His buddy did not die. Everything continues perfectly.

That is not something one mentally believes. He must come to it on his own, through soul-knowing people, animals and plants that scream "Life!" louder than his memory of the IED.

No matter how many times we relive a past painful event, the bottom line is this: it brought us to this beginning moment where we have the choice to choose to love what happened as perfect, just how it was, and to be more wisely guarded. We either choose to do that and evolve to a higher level of heaven, or we devolve into more self-and other-destroying darkness. We cannot regret our way out of regret, or worry our way out of worries, and we cannot believe our way out of darkness, or suppress our feelings and thoughts to get out. We can only love-guard our way out. The choice to be love rather than to be regret/worried/falsely excited can be the most courageous act that we perform.

For some, that is a very tough journey to make. However, those are the leaders who will show the rest of us the way.

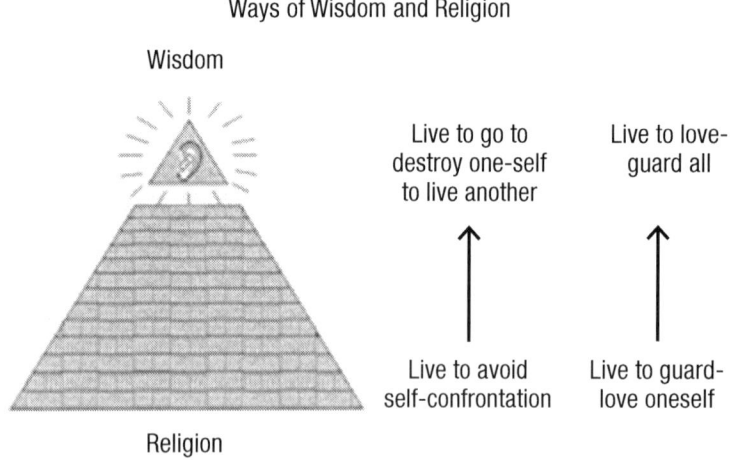

"And if he should be troubled, he will come to marvel." If he should be troubled and then, evolve out of it, he will marvel.

When we release ourselves from the past and future and become again in the beginning, experiencing movement from stillness and our real selves, it can be the ultimate high. People describe "transcendence" in many ways: Some say: "I feel I have become again," or "I sense that I have moved to a new level of wonderful living," or "I am full of energy and insight," or "I now look back on what seemed so horrible and see it as a gift."

Sometimes, transcendence accompanies a sense of being one with all, being clear, being more independent, being creative, being in-touch, being more alive, being more love-guarded, and being fulfilled. Those on the Way of Wisdom crave troubles and its release to transcendence as addicts crave heroin.

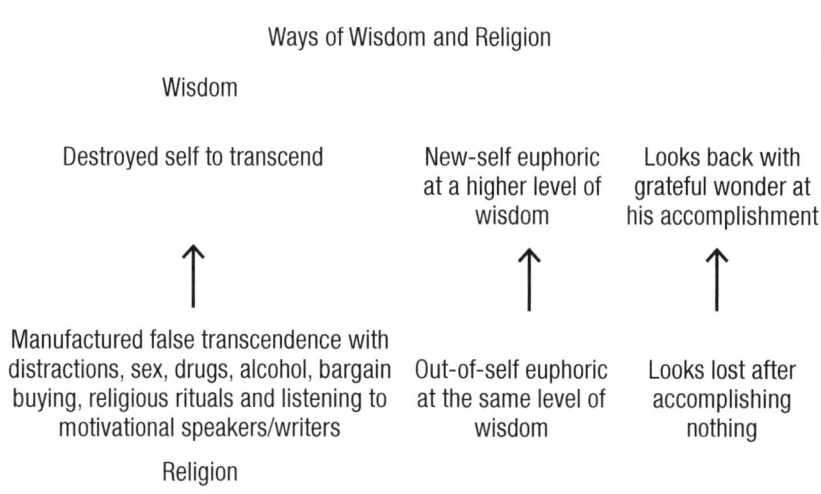

"And marveling, he will come to reign over all." After one comes to marvel, one possesses the clarity and wisdom to navigate life much more wisely.

Pity the unwise who confronts a person who has suffered so much to reign. That lion or lioness will eat that man alive.

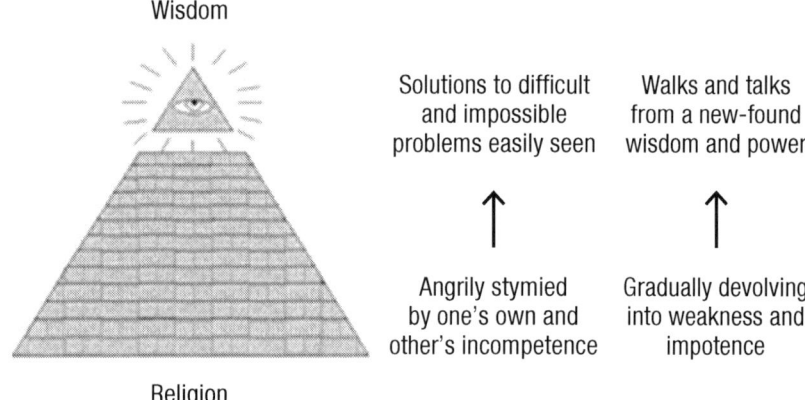

"And reigning, he will come to be still with all." The person who rules at a higher level also rests at a higher level in his new-found awareness. He may be found hand in hand with someone he loves walking in stillness, or chatting with someone sensitively and slowly, or simply sitting in a park watching the leaves blow in the wind knowing that the universe has just been reset for him.

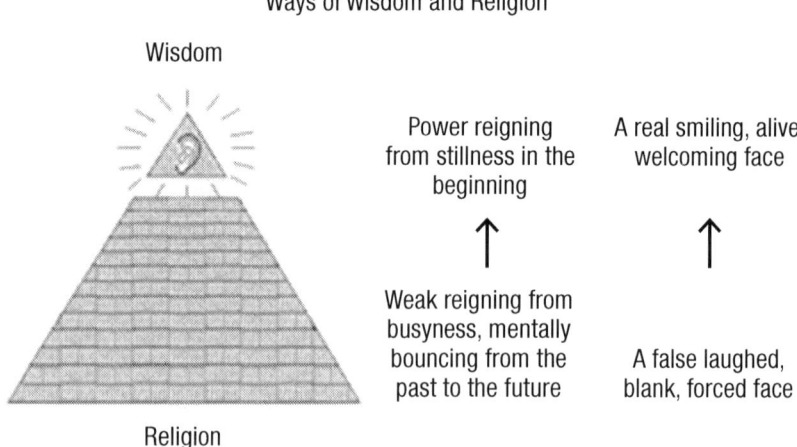

On the Way of Wisdom, one seeks more than "opposite" experiences. He seeks "higher-dimensional" experiences.

Jesus' Five Steps to Sanity and Fulfillment

- **Step One**: Seeks an experience which tells him he has chosen regret, worry, and false-excitement, rather than stillness in the beginning.

- **Step Two**: Seeks the experience of self-confrontation with the ways he has chosen to be weak and false.

- **Step Three**: Seeks the experience of wonder when he has released himself from the grip of false solutions.

- **Step Four**: Seeks the experience of being a more powerful ruler over himself and his interactions with others.

- **Step Five**: Seeks the experience of resting more powerfully in a deeper stillness in the beginning.

The bottom line: What we seek is what we find, live, enjoy or suffer.

CHAPTER SEVEN

PAUL'S SELF-DEVELOPMENT METHOD

Be Saved by Your Faith in Paul's Gospel

We left Paul outside of Jerusalem, on his way to find non-Jews outside of Israel who would adopt his gospel. We saw that Paul concluded that the redemption of humankind involved two steps: reconciliation and salvation. God fulfilled the first step when, according to Paul, but not according to Jesus, He lovingly sent his Son, Jesus, in the likeness of human sinful flesh to sacrifice himself on the cross. When that happened, God ceased to be an enemy of humankind.

However, according to Paul, humankind must acknowledge Jesus' sacrifice in order to be saved. They do that by believing in Paul's "gospel of God," not by following Jesus' Way, and not by following the Torah's laws. He says in Romans 3:28:

> *For we hold that a man is justified by faith apart from works of law.*

"For we hold that a man is justified by faith apart from works of law." We believe that a man is saved by his faith in my (Paul's) gospel and not by anything he does.

In other words, a person becomes one again with God (saved), as he was before Adam's sin, when he trusts in Paul's ideas about Jesus, the same ideas that Jesus never believed in or lived.

Paul makes no logical sense. He tells people to believe in the Son of God, who contradicted Paul, in order to be united with the Son of God.

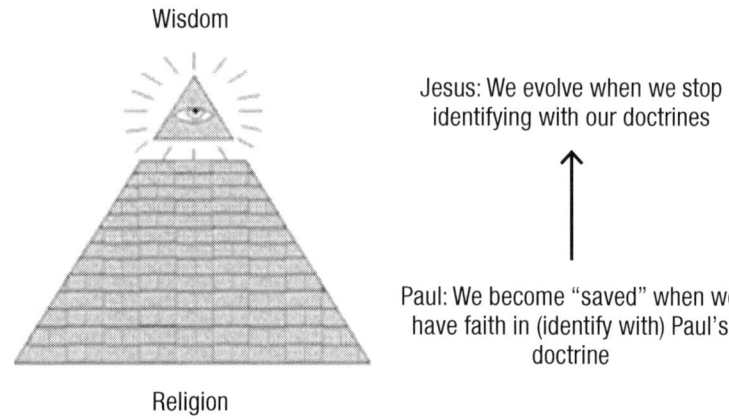

Avoid Evil Deeds

Paul then contradicts himself in Galatians 5:19-21:

> *Now the works of the flesh are plain: fornication, impurity, licentiousness, idolatry, sorcery, enmity, strife, jealousy, anger, selfishness, dissension, party spirit, envy, drunkenness, carousing, and the like. I warn you, as I warned you before, that those who do such things shall not inherit the kingdom of God.*

"I warn you, as I warned you before, that those who do such things shall not inherit the kingdom of God." I am warning you again, obey the laws or you will not be saved.

Paul changed his theology. At first, a person was "saved" through faith alone. He then retracted that notion, claiming that there are things a person must *do* in addition to having faith.

Obey Paul's Laws

Paul even gets quite specific about how a person should behave, especially toward women, as we see in 1 Cor. 11: 3-8:

> But I want you to understand that the head of every man is Christ, the head of a woman is her husband, and the head of Christ is God...but any woman who prays or prophesies with her head unveiled dishonors her head -- it is the same as if her head were shaven. For if a woman will not veil herself, then she should cut off her hair; but if it is disgraceful for a woman to be shorn or shaven, let her wear a veil. For a man ought not to cover his head, since he is the image and glory of God; but woman is the glory of man. For man was not made from woman, but woman from man...That is why a woman ought to have a veil on her head, because of the angels.

In this passage, Paul sets up a hierarchy of authority, again, that implies a lack of logic.

The topmost authority is Jesus, who never made any pronouncements about women like those of Paul.

A husband must follow the laws of Jesus, which Paul does not disclose. Instead, he discloses his own laws.

No one could possibly live as Paul requires. You cannot follow Christ when you do not know what he said, and when you are told to obey laws that he never declared.

Ways of Wisdom and Religion

Wisdom

Jesus: You have one core law: Be congruent with your real self

Paul: Obey Christ's laws by obeying mine.

Religion

Do Good

Many people associate Jesus with ordering his followers to do good deeds for others. He actually spoke little about that, as we have seen so far. He left it up to individuals to soul-know how to love-guard all.

Note well: In Rom. 12: 9-21, Paul spoke the commands that people associate with Jesus:

> *Let love be genuine; hate what is evil, hold fast to what is good; love one another with brotherly affection; outdo one another in showing honor. Never flag in zeal, be aglow with the Spirit, serve the Lord. Rejoice in your hope, be patient in tribulation, be constant in prayer. Contribute to the needs of the saints, practice hospitality.*

> *Bless those who persecute you; bless and do not curse them. Rejoice with those who rejoice, weep with those who weep. Live in harmony with one another; do not be haughty, but associate with the lowly; never be conceited. Repay no one evil for evil, but take thought for what is noble in the sight of all. If possible, so far as it depends upon you, live peaceably with all.*

> *Beloved, never avenge yourselves, but leave it to the wrath of God; for it is written, "Vengeance is mine, I will repay, says the Lord." (Deut. 32:35) No, "if your enemy is hungry, feed him; if he is thirsty, give him drink; for by so doing you will heap burning coals upon his head." (Proverbs 25:21-22) Do not be overcome by evil, but overcome evil with good.*

"Let love be genuine." Do not pretend to love, but do it honestly.

"Hate what is evil." Hate evil actions and thoughts.

"Hold fast to what is good." Remain in accord with Paul's notions of "good."

"Love one another with brotherly affection." Love your neighbor.

"Outdo one another in showing honor." Do not be content to be average in honoring God.

"Never flag in zeal." Remain steadfast in the intensity of your faith.

"Be aglow with the Spirit, serve the Lord." Be radiant in your connection with God.

"Rejoice in your hope." Rejoice in your hope that by living according to Paul's doctrine, you will be saved.

"Be patient in tribulation." Be patient when others persecute you for the way you live.

"Be constant in prayer." Continually be one with God.

"Contribute to the needs of the saints." Support those who are recognized as living by Paul's doctrine.

"Practice hospitality." Welcome people to your homes.

"Bless those who persecute you; bless and do not curse them." Make holy those who persecute you; do not hate them.

"Rejoice with those who rejoice, weep with those who weep." Rejoice and weep with good and bad people equally, no matter the reasons for their rejoicing and weeping.

"Live in harmony with one another." Be peaceful with one another.

"Do not be haughty, but associate with the lowly." Do not be arrogant, but associate with those who are overlooked by others and/or who do not assert themselves.

"Never be conceited." Do not be vain.

"Repay no one evil for evil, but take thought for what is noble in the sight of all." Do not do what I define as "bad" to those who do bad things to you or to others.

"If possible, so far as it depends upon you, live peaceably with all." Live in peace with people who do loving and unloving things.

"Beloved, never avenge yourselves, but leave it to the wrath of God; for it is written, 'Vengeance is mine, I will repay, says the Lord.'" (Deut. 32:35). Do not seek revenge. God will visit his wrath upon those who harm you.

"If your enemy is hungry, feed him; if he is thirsty, give him drink; for by so doing you will heap burning coals upon his head." Give food and drink to your enemy if he is in need; for by doing so, you will humble him.

"Do not be overcome by evil, but overcome evil with good." Stand up to those who do not live Paul's doctrine by living it fully yourself.

Many people associate those statements with Jesus, however, Jesus never left such a list of guidelines or laws.

Paul desired to control the thinking and behavior of people, while Jesus did not.

Paul commanded people to love; Jesus taught people to love-guard.

Paul asked people to be peaceful, Jesus expected his disciples to be "fire, sword, and war" in the world.

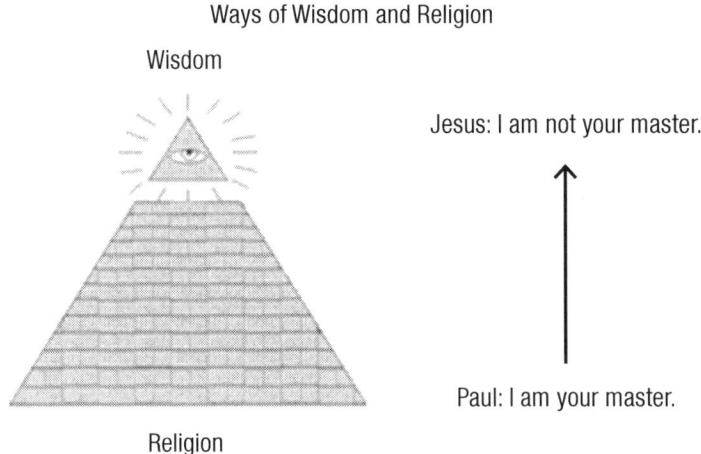

INDOCTRINATE NON-BELIEVERS

Paul's command to ensure the continuance of his legacy is stated in 1 Cor. 4:14-16:

> *I do not write this to make you ashamed, but to admonish you as my beloved children. For though you have countless guides in Christ, you do not have many fathers. For I became your father in Christ Jesus through the gospel. I urge you, then, be imitators of me.*

"I do not write this to make you ashamed, but to admonish you as my beloved children." I write to you to scold you as a parent to a child, because you have not done as I told you to do.

"For though you have countless guides in Christ, you do not have many fathers, for I became your father in Christ Jesus through the gospel." I am your father, that is, your ultimate authority, even when you are guided by Christ.

"I urge you, then, be imitators of me." Teach exactly what I taught you.

That may be the strongest statement of Paul's desire to be the ultimate authority over the thoughts and behavior of everyone in his church. He had no intention of freeing people to use soul-knowing to make decisions for themselves. He desired to control every aspect of their lives, while manipulating them into thinking that they did the will of Jesus, and through him, the will of God.

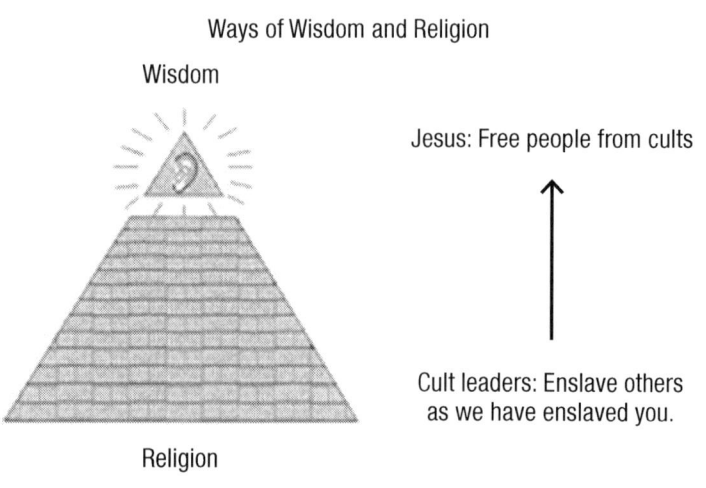

Cult leaders are everywhere today. Jesus spoke of them in Chapter 20, Poem One (Saying 102):

Woe to them,

The Pharisees,[1]

For
they
resemble
a dog[2]

He
resting,[3]

[1] *Pharisees*: Those who indoctrinate rather than teach people how to listen and discover their own hidden wisdom.

[2] *Dog*: The lowest of the low in character. Dogs gathered at the garbage dumps to eat.

[3] *Resting*: Not laboring to soul-know and discover the meaning of what he heard.

*He
upon the manger⁴
of some oxen.⁵*

*For
he
eats⁶
not,⁷*

*And
he
permits
not the oxen
to eat.⁸*

⁴*Manger*: Place where people go to get their answers.

⁵*Oxen*: People on the Way of Religion. Those not discovering hidden wisdom.

⁶*Eats*: Soul-knows and integrates what he hears.

⁷*For he eats not*: The indoctrinators do not soul-know; and thus, do not live from He Who Lives.

⁸*He permits not the oxen to eat*: Indoctrinators hinder people who are inspired with ideas that differ from the group's doctrine by telling them that they are wrong. In that way, they force people to conform to the group's Way.

Ways of Wisdom and Religion

Jesus: Eat the wisdom that is revealed to you

Cult leaders: Eat from our hand

Ways of Wisdom and Religion

Wisdom

Jesus: Love-guard people who identify with doctrines

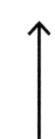

Indoctrinators: Demonize people who disagree with "our" official doctrine

Religion

CHAPTER EIGHT

THE RESULTS OF LIVING JESUS' WAY OF WISDOM

INTRODUCTION

If we were to ask people today, "What picture comes to your mind when you think of a person who follows Jesus' Way perfectly," they would probably describe Mary, the mother of Jesus, or a saint.

Jesus, on the other hand, would present the picture of a mountain. Yes, a mountain.

Let us explore why.

A Mountain

Twice in the Gospel, Jesus repeats the Mountain Poem. In it, he announces the importance of us becoming a mountain.

The first instance of the Mountain Poem is in the centerpiece of the Gospel, Chapter 11. It is Poem Three (Saying 48) of that Chapter:

Jesus said this:	[1]*Should two*: Two beings in one person, one's real self and God.

Should
two[1]
*make peace
with each other*[2]
in this house[3]
unified,[4]

They
will speak
to the mountain
this:[5,6]

"*Move,*"[7]

And
it
will move.[8]

[2]*Should two make peace with each other*: Should a person follow the Way of Wisdom and become congruent with God, such that they possess the same life, power and Light intelligence.

[3]*House*: A person.

[4]*Should two make peace... unified*: Should two who have been battling become one.

[5]*Mountain*: A person who lives in powerful stillness, standing high on his own feet above all others.

[6]*Should...they will speak to the mountain this*: Should a person in oneness with They-who-live-within say to himself:

[7]*Move*: Be movement from stillness.

[8]*It will move*: The still person will move in the world.

"Should two make peace with each other in this house unified." Should two parts of oneself, the false self and the real self, become one in a person…

When we think of an evolved, powerful, independent person, we may think of someone whose strength arises from his physical prowess, his intelligence, his experience, or his money. At times, we may think of a person of character; however, do we go further and describe to ourselves what gives a person character.

Jesus did reflect on character. He concluded that an evolved person was one who had become congruent with himself, in other words, one who made peace between his false self and his real self. One does that, when one acknowledges his false self, but acts from his real self.

"They will speak to the mountain this:" In the Bible, a "mountain" is an evolved person. When an author describes someone as "going up on the mountain," he means that the person goes high up within himself to communicate directly with God through soul-knowing. Therefore, one goal of this Gospel is to enable every person to go up on the mountain and communicate directly with his source of inspiration.

Everyone does that at times. For example, when an artist goes to a special environment to be still and receive insights, he goes high up on the mountain to communicate with God. He may not call God, "God," but what he calls his source of inspiration is not important.

Jesus recognized that a mountain was the perfect symbol for a person who has become congruent with his real self. He is self-contained; he speaks from the core life that Jesus found divine. He has become a mountain of a person.

"They will speak to the mountain this: 'Move,' and it will move." The tangible sign of a person who is one with his divine Light is movement from stillness. That person is still in the world, like the images we see of the Buddha. However, that person also moves in the world.

A person, who is very still and powerful is for Jesus, like a mountain. He was in awe that such stillness could move. So, a mountain became his symbol for an evolved person, not a person with a halo.

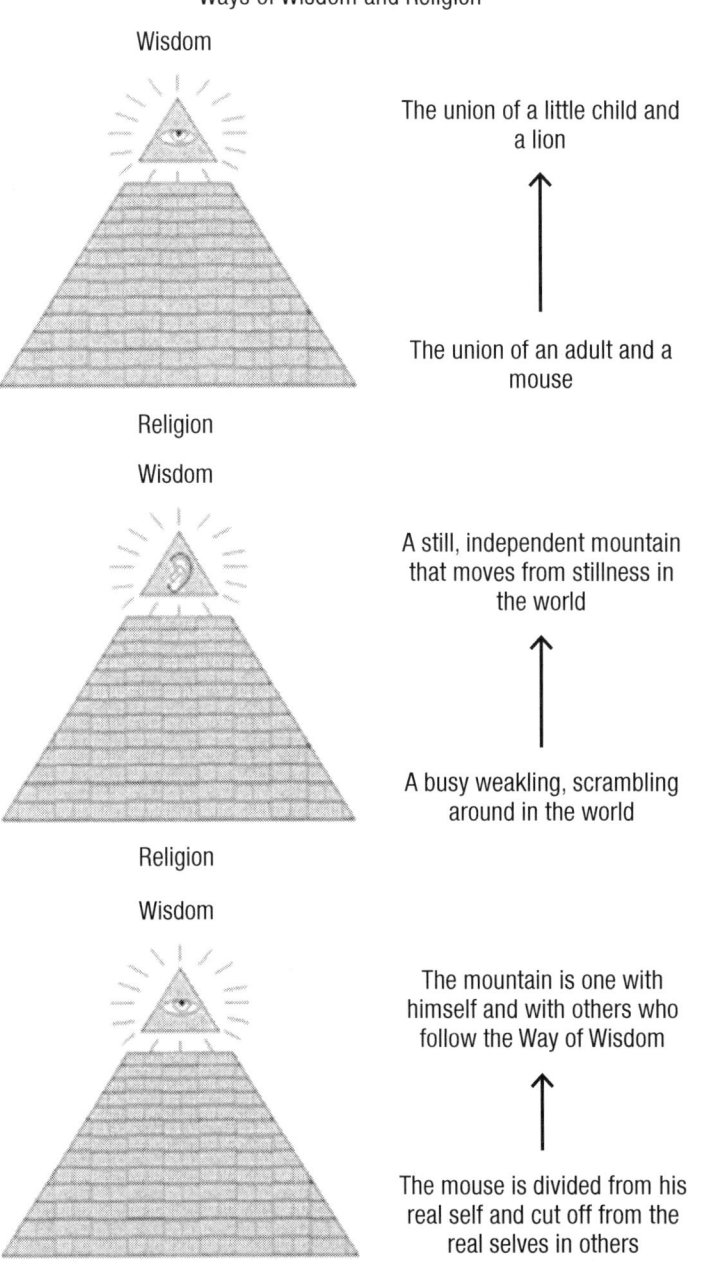

A Kingdom

Jesus also used the metaphor of the kingdom to describe a person who has evolved on his Way. In Chapter 21, Poem Seven (Saying 113), Jesus indicates that many such kingdoms exist unseen, and that they are spreading:

His disciples
asked him:

"The kingdom,[1,2]

It
is coming
on which day?"[3]

Jesus
responded:

"The kingdom,
comes
not in watching.[4]

They[5]
will say
not this:
'Behold here,'
or
'Behold there.'[6]

[1] *Kingdom*: For Jesus, an environment ruled by an individual to the degree that he is one with himself.

[2] *Kingdom*: For the disciples, Palestine after the Messiah drives out the Romans and restores it in the likeness of David's kingdom.

[3] *Day*: A time when the Messiah will drive the invaders out of Israel. A time when the Messiah would cleanse the temple, and bring everyone to worship the one true God.

[4] *The kingdom comes not in watching*: The kingdom will not come because you disciples stand around watching for what you could not and will not recognize.

[5] *They*: People on the Way of Religion.

[6] *They will not say, "behold here" or "behold there:"* They will not see what they are expecting.

*Rather
the kingdom
of the Father
is spreading
upon the earth,⁷*

*And
men⁸
peer
not upon it.⁹*

⁷*Upon the earth*: Upon the reflective consciousness in people following the Way of Wisdom.

⁸*Men*: Those following the Way of Religion.

⁹*Peer not upon it*: Cannot see what is right in front of them.

Ways of Wisdom and Religion

Wisdom

Religion

The light kingdom seen in others by those living light

The light kingdom unseen by those living darkness

Wisdom

Religion

The kingdom exists today in the consciousness of some people

The kingdom does not exist today because we cannot see it

A Twin

Jesus also says that those who have evolved on his Way become twins. The Prologue (Saying One) states that:

Poem One
These
   are
the words...
 	
Which...
   Jesus...
     spoke.[1]
 	
Poem Two
   And
    he
wrote them,
 	
Namely
  the twin[2]
Judas,[3,4]
 	
  Also
  called
  "Twin."[5]
	[1]These are the words... which Jesus spoke: These are the wisdom poems that Jesus composed.
	
	[2]*The Twin*: In the text, we find the Greek word, "Didymus," meaning, "twin."
	
	[3]*Judas*: Jesus had two disciples named Judas.
	
	[4]*And he wrote...Judas*: Judas, also called Thomas, wrote the poems down as Jesus' scribe.
	
	[5]*Twin*: In the text, we find the Aramaic word, "Thomas," meaning, "twin." Judas was also called Thomas or Twin. Therefore, we know that this Judas had a twin brother or sister.

"These are the words which Jesus spoke." These are the wisdom words that Jesus spoke.

  "And he wrote them, namely, the twin Judas, also called "Twin." And Judas, called "Twin," wrote down Jesus' words.

When Jesus used "twin" twice in the same poem in such a strange manner, and when that Poem occurs in the Prologue, he points to the fact that this Gospel is about becoming a twin, as Judas did. That is a deliberate, carefully-constructed sentence.

The author never uses the word, "twin" again in the Gospel; however, he defines a person who is fully evolved on the Way of Wisdom as a twin in other manners. For example, in the Child poem, he says: "they will come to be single ones." He means as people evolve on to be little children again, they will each become congruent who he is at his core, divine life. In other words, one becomes a twin of God.

Above, we read that a person becomes a twin of himself when he makes peace between his false self and his real self. In Chapter 21, Poem Two (Saying 106), Jesus says that a person also makes peace with others by becoming their twin. Below, not especially that the word "you" is plural.

When you (pl) should make the two the one[1]	[1] *When you (pl) should make the two the one*: When you people should become one with the divine life in each of you.
You (pl) will come to be, the sons of Man.[2]	[2] *You will come to be sons of Man*. You will become sons of God.

In that context, to "make the two, the one" means one is to become the twin of everyone, because all have the same core life.

Jesus defined "sons of Man" in a previous Poem Five that we studied from Chapter Two (Saying 3b):

When
you
should know yourselves;

Then
they
will know you,

And
you
will realize

That
you
are
sons
of the Father.

The phrase "sons of Man" in the former Poem parallels "sons of the Father" in the latter. (That is the way the Semitic authors define their terms.) Thus, we know that in this Gospel, "sons of Man" means "sons of the Father." Further, when we combine what we know from the "Mother" poems, we know that "sons of Man" means "sons of the Father and Mother."

The Gospel came to be called the Gospel of Thomas. Because "Thomas" means "twin," the original name of the Gospel was probably intended to be understood as the "Gospel of the Twin."

Ways of Wisdom and Religion

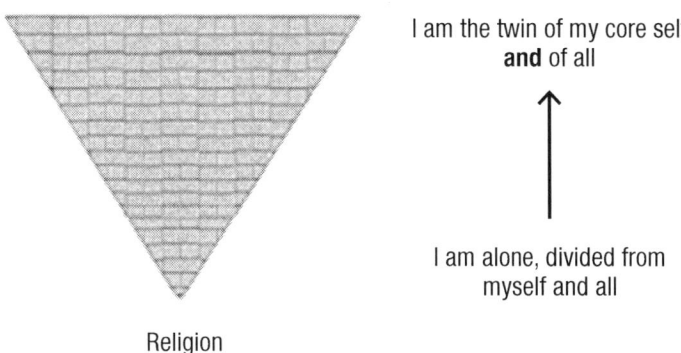

An Empty One

Jesus also thought of a person who has become fulfilled on his Way as a person who is empty. Such a person must become empty like a cup in order to become full on the Way of Wisdom. Jesus tells us that in Chapter 19, Poem Three (Saying 97):

*The kingdom
of the Father,*

*It
is comparable
to a woman
bearing a jar,*[1]

*It
full of meal,*[2]

*She
walking on a way,*[3]

*It
far away.*[4]
*The ear
of the jar
broke,*[5]

[1] *Jar*: What contains our false selves. We call it the "ego."

[2] *Meal*: False identifications that we consume.

[3] *She walking on a way*: She transitioning from the Way of Religion to the Way of Wisdom.

[4] *It far away*: It being a long journey.

[5] *The ear of the jar broke*: One of ego's ears broke. In other words, a person deliberately stopped listening with their [2] ears and began soul-listening with their third ear.

*And
the meal
emptied out*[6]
*after her
along the way,*

*And
she
knew
not what
was happening,*[7]

*And
she
did
not realize any trouble.*[8]

*When
she
opened inward
to her house,*[9]

*She
released the jar
down,*[9]

*And
she
discovered it
being
empty.*[11]

[6]*And the meal emptied out*: Her false selves fell upon the earth, without her even realizing it, so focused was she on her path (of soul-listening).

[7]*And she knew not what was happening*: And as she enjoyed becoming more alive and wise, she did not notice that her false selves were leaving her.

[8]*And she did not realize any trouble*: Like a woman after she gave birth, she did not realize the trouble, because of the joys she was experiencing.

[9]*When she opened inward to her house*: When she reflected on who she had become.

[10]*She released the jar down*: She emptied her ego.

[11]*And she discovered it being empty*: Her ego was empty.

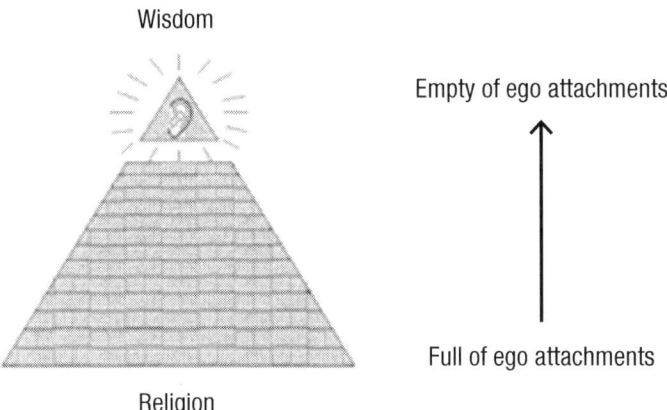

INVULNERABILITY

As a mountain is invulnerable, so Jesus viewed an evolved person. Those following his Way will discover themselves blessed, but hated and persecuted--and love it. They react positively to attacks because they have become invulnerable. Jesus tells us why in Chapter 1, Poem Three (Saying 68):

*Jesus
said this:*

*You
are
the best ones[1]*

*When
they[2]
hate you[3]*

*And
persecute you;[4]*

*For
they
will discover
not any place[5]*

[1] *Blest ones*: People one with their core divine life.

[2] *They*: People on the Way of Religion.

[3] *When they hate you*: When they hate you for being the children of God.

[4] *And persecute you*: And make life difficult for you.

[5] *Place*: A vulnerable spot within you that can be exploited to control your thinking and behavior.

Where
you
have
*not persecuted yourselves.*⁶

⁶*For they will discover not any place where you have not persecuted yourselves*: They will not find a weakness in your character that you have not examined and transcended.

Ways of Wisdom and Religion

Wisdom

Invulnerable — He identifies with nothing that can be attacked and exploited

↑ ↑

Vulnerable — He identifies with what can be attacked and exploited

Religion

A Child and a Lion

We saw previously that Jesus told us that on his Way we would return to the childlike kingdom in which we were born. That is the kingdom marked by congruence with oneself. He also visualized a person becoming a lion that would not permit indoctrinators to seduce him into following the Way of Religion. Thus, Jesus' evolved person is the seemingly contradictory characteristics of being both a child who loves all and a lion that guards himself from all:

CHAPTER NINE

THE RESULTS OF LIVING PAUL'S WAY OF RELIGION

Salvation and Righteousness

Paul created a doctrine-based gospel and staked his life and legacy on everyone believing it. To ensure that they complied, he interwove his letters with intangible rewards for his acolytes. In Romans 1:16-17 we read:

> *For I am not ashamed of the gospel, because it is the power of God that brings salvation to everyone who believes: first to the Jew, then to the Gentile. For in the gospel the righteousness of God is revealed—a righteousness that is by faith from first to last, just as it is written: "The righteous will live by faith."*

"For I am not ashamed of the gospel, because it is the power of God that brings salvation to everyone who believes." I am not ashamed of my gospel (not the gospel of Jesus), because it is the power of God that brings salvation to everyone that believes.

As we saw above, Jesus had a different gospel. Further, he never said that one must believe it word for word. Rather, he said, one to live it in his own way by following his inspiration. Jesus laid out a process for personal development, not a doctrine to be believed. He knew that people could believe in a creed and not be changed by it.

"**It...brings salvation to everyone who believes: first to the Jew, then to the Gentile.**" The gospel favors the Jews over the Gentiles when it comes time for God to reward believers.

According to Paul, we are not all equal. Race and traditions determine one's essential value in God's eyes. Some people are more favored for salvation than others.

"**For in the gospel the righteousness of God is revealed—a righteousness that is by faith from first to last, just as it is written: 'The righteous will live by faith.'**" One experiences the "righteousness of God" through his faith in Paul's doctrine.

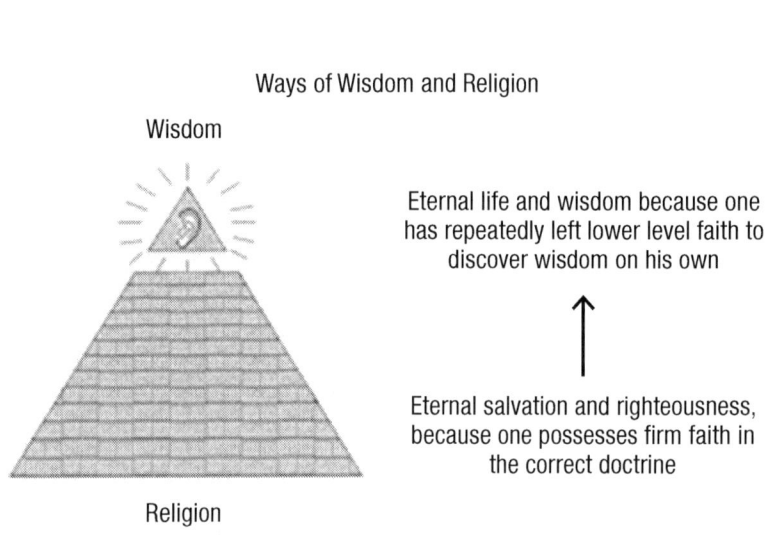

Trouble and Distress

Paul believes that he loves everyone equally but he contradicts himself in his letters, as we see in the next chapter of the same letter to the Romans 2:9-10):

> *There will be trouble and distress for every human being who does evil: first for the Jew, then for the Gentile; but glory, honor and peace for everyone who does good: first for the Jew, then for the Gentile.*

"There will be trouble and distress for every human being who does evil: first for the Jew, then for the Gentile; but glory, honor and peace for everyone who does good." There will be trouble and distress for everyone in the world (starting with the Jews) who do not adopt Paul's gospel. On the other hand, there will be eternal "honor and peace" (starting with Jews) for those who live it.

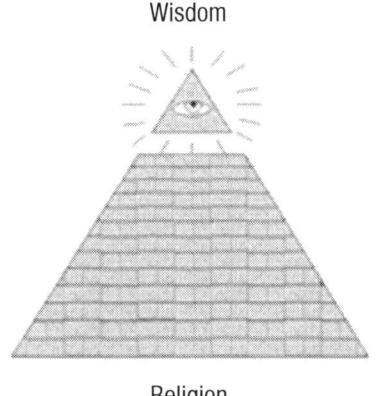

Ways of Wisdom and Religion

Wisdom

We experience the level of life and wisdom that we possess until we evolve or devolve

Eternal trouble and distress for those not living under the correct doctrine; eternal honor and peace for those who live it

Religion

Inherit the Kingdom

For Jesus, the kingdom is a state of soul-knowing oneself, others, and the nature of the world. As a person evolves, he becomes a higher level of heavenly kingdom.

As we see below in 2 Thes.1: 5-11, for Paul, the kingdom is a place we enter after we die, and brought to the world when Jesus returns for the second time.

> *This is evidence of the righteous judgment of God, that you may be made worthy of the kingdom of God, for which you are suffering; since indeed God deems it just to repay with affliction those who afflict you, and to grant rest with us to you who are afflicted, when the Lord Jesus is revealed from heaven with his mighty angels in flaming*

fire, inflicting vengeance upon those who do not know God and upon those who do not obey the gospel of our Lord Jesus. They shall suffer the punishment of eternal destruction and exclusion from the presence of the Lord and from the glory of his might, when he comes on that day to be glorified in his saints, and to be marveled at in all who have believed, because our testimony to you was believed. To this end we always pray for you, that our God may make you worthy of his call, and may fulfill every good resolve and work of faith by his power.

"This is evidence of the righteous judgment of God, that you may be made worthy of the kingdom of God, for which you are suffering."

God will recognize your suffering and make you "worthy of the kingdom of God" at the end of times.

For Jesus, the kingdom is lived at a higher level of heavenly knowing now, not later. We suffer now to evolve, and to live the rewards now, not after we die.

"Since indeed God deems it just to repay with affliction those who afflict you, and to grant rest with us to you who are afflicted, when the Lord Jesus is revealed from heaven with his mighty angels in flaming fire inflicting vengeance upon those who do not know God and upon those who do not obey the gospel of our Lord Jesus."

In the future the God, Jesus, will descend to the world from heaven with his mighty angels. At that time, God will afflict vengeance upon those who have afflicted you, who did not know God, and who did not obey Paul's gospel. Those who have been faithful will be spared further affliction.

As you saw, Jesus did not experience God as vengeful. He did not say that God will punish those who do not believe in his wisdom poems, nor those who do not follow his Way. Jesus teaches that one suffers in the natural order of things when he does not evolve.

"They shall suffer the punishment of eternal destruction and exclusion from the presence of the Lord and from the glory of his might, when he comes on that day to be glorified in his saints, and to be marveled at in all who have believed, because our testimony to you was believed."

Those who have not followed Paul's gospel will suffer the punishment of eternal destruction and exclusion from the presence of Jesus and his glory when he comes from heaven to earth. At that time, Jesus will be glorified by those who have remained faithful to Paul's gospel, who in turn, will be admired by those who have not been faithful.

The Jesus we saw in the Poems above would get sick to his stomach to hear Paul's words. He did not develop an after-death carrot-stick motivational system. He would not indoctrinate people with a fear of something that they have never experienced. Instead, he pointed to the present outcomes of not living as light, life, and wisdom.

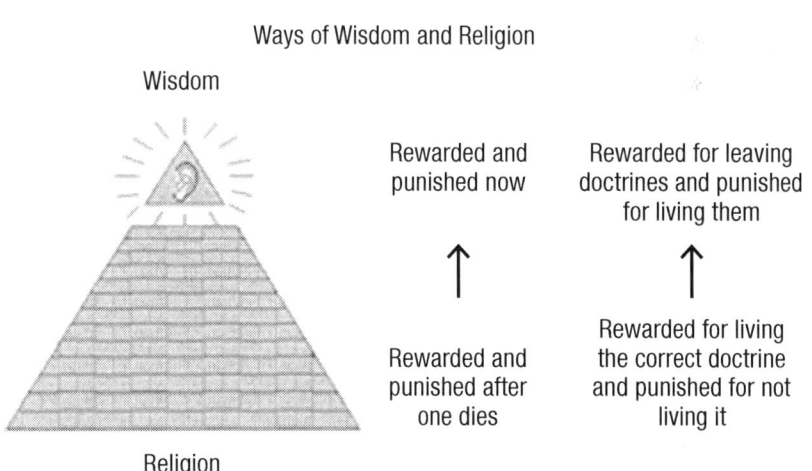

Ways of Wisdom and Religion

Wisdom

Religion

Jesus: Responsible for service to the poor, ill, disabled, aged, and disenfranchised no matter their identification with doctrine

↑

Paul: Responsible for the psychological and physical persecution and killing of people who did not conform to his doctrine

Wisdom

Religion

Jesus and those unseen & unheralded who may never have known him

↓
↑

Hitler, Stalin, Nationalists, Elitists, Media-idols, King David, Paul, Mohamed, the Vatican, Dalai Lamas and others heralded for causing division between people

CHAPTER TEN

CONCLUSIONS

What We Know About the Author of Thomas

From the previous chapters, we have come to know a great deal about the author of the Gospel of Thomas; let us consider this knowledge now:

1. **The author was probably a Jew**: He knew the Old Testament metaphors, such as "kingdom" and "mountain," and the meaning of the allegories, such as that about the Garden of Eden and Moses' sojourn in the wilderness.

2. **The author neither adhered to nor supported the Torah, the Jewish traditions, or the Jewish authorities**: In fact, he attacked them as idols.

3. **The author was a poet, not a theologian like Paul**: The author studied people and nature and then arrived at the principles governing human interaction and evolution. He did not use his mind or mystical experiences to understand things that cannot be verified by others. He would never, for example, ask people to believe in the Trinity, if that concept of God could not be experienced.

4. **He saw the Way of Religion as darkness, and the Way of Wisdom as Light**: He did not endorse any theological or secular religion. He did not support pledging allegiance to a flag, an economic system, a spouse, a job, a celebrity, an organization, or a belief system. He rode one horse, that of the Light found in all; he pulled one bow, the desire to be the twin of every person; he followed one leader, the One that guided him through soul-knowing.

5. **The author studied with Jesus or he was Jesus:** He knew well some of the parables and sayings of Jesus that we find in the New Testament. Further, he understood them in their more primitive versions; that is, closer to the way their author composed them.

6. **The author composed a unified Gospel:** The Gospel of Thomas is not simply a collection of sayings. It communicates a unified philosophy. The author consistently used metaphors in the same way throughout. The logic holds together to elucidate a single core theme with many sub-themes.

7. **The author was a wise therapist:** He saw the cause of emotional torment in a person, and he articulated a unified path to self-development.

8. **The author was a wise statesman:** He saw that religion divided nations, and he showed how to unite them.

9. **The author was probably murdered:** Palestine in the first century was ruled through an informal agreement between the Roman occupiers and their Jewish collaborators. They did not want an uprising to destroy that relationship and what it brought them. The Poems in Thomas attack all indoctrinators, and Jewish leaders by title. One would not live long in first century Palestine while publicly calling the elite "dogs."

10. **The author composed the Gospel of Thomas to proclaim the solution for world peace should he die:** It is inconceivable to think that a person who: saw the world's troubles as clearly as the author of Thomas; gathered 128 wisdom poems, some of which we know that Jesus composed; composed others; and knew that he could be killed at any time, would not compose a Book to ensure that his message lived on after him.

11. **The author lived love-guarded:** He would have been compassionate to both the suffering and not-suffering alike,

while holding everyone responsible for their thinking and behavior. He would have been a walking love-guard that posed a threat to everyone, even his closest friends.

12. **The author would have affected people over great distances.** He did not compose all of his poems in a single sitting. He would have composed one, edited it, recited it, and edited it again. He would have done that repeatedly until satisfied. Meanwhile, people would have memorized one poem after another and communicated them to others, and they to others. In that way, over many years, knowledge of this radical, wise person and his radical gospel would have spread over a great area, and likely to other countries when his poems were memorized and recited by traders.

13. **The author had a following of disciples and enemies.** The author of Thomas lived these poems. He would have attracted people seeking wisdom, and he would have upset the conformists in the society around him.

14. **The author was not interested in self-importance:** He did not say that he was the Messiah or "the Son of God." He did not want to be anyone's master. He desired only for people to honor the core divine life in themselves and others. He did everything possible to empower people to evolve in wisdom.

15. **We would know about such an author:** No one with such a large following of both disciples and enemies, and with such a huge portfolio of wisdom poems, could have vanished from the historical record.

16. **After the author died, his followers would have divided into different schools of interpretation of his poems.** One does not leave the Way of Religion to follow the Way of Wisdom quickly or easily. For example, in the past 50 years, scholars, clerics and lay people have studied the Gospel of Thomas; yet, no one has seen the Way of Wisdom in it, because they have been blinded by their Way of Religion beliefs.

That must have also been true at the time that the author lived. Few, if anyone, truly grasped his radical message. To make it more difficult for people to transform themselves in the 1st century, economic conditions were very difficult and the average life expectancy was about 35 years. Few people would have had the time and luxury of abandoning their preoccupation with survival in order to seek wisdom.

Thus, because it took time, courage, and resources to leave the Way of Religion for the Way of Wisdom, many schools of interpretation of his ideas would have arisen after the author's death. Each would have created a collection, or even a Gospel of his poems to support their different philosophies and theologies.

Most schools would twist his Way into a belief-based religion. That would do two things: First, members could feel above others because of their belief in the Truth; and secondly, members could substitute the long, hard work of spiritual growth for quick and easy beliefs.

Other schools would integrate the author's ideas into the school of Judaism that they already practiced. We can imagine many people saying something like, "Let's not throw the baby out with the bathwater," when that is exactly what the author was doing.

It's likely that the leader of at least one school of thought would have been so outraged and threatened by the author's poems that he attempted to erase all memory of them. He would do so by refusing to quote them, and by claiming that the author was the center of his theology.

We know that all of this happened after Jesus's death.

17. **The author's Book would have been hidden**. The author threatened everyone; almost certainly, nearly everyone rejected him and his message. He ultimately lived alone with his God, as all great people do. He was probably killed by his enemies. Anyone with his Gospel on hand would

have suffered the same fate; therefore, only a few copies would have been made, and those would have been read in secret. It seems more likely that it was lost to most people. Certainly, the 4th century Bishops of the Church of Peter and Paul, who decided on the works to be included in the New Testament, ignored and denigrated Thomas.

18. **The Author Intricately Organized the Gospel of Thomas:** I will present that organization in Volume Two and the succeeding books. After reading them, you are likely to agree that only one person who intimately understood every poem and how each fit with the others to convey a unified Gospel could have done it.

Who Authored the Gospel of Thomas?

The evidence points to Jesus as the most likely author of the Gospel of Thomas. We know of no one else that matches those 18 conditions.

What Do We Know About the Messiah?

Many people were anointed as "Messiah" in the Old Testament. However, some prophesies pointed to two special ones who would appear that that would bring peace to Israel and the world. We can read in Zechariah 6:13:

> *It is he who shall build the temple of the Lord and shall bear royal honor, and shall sit and rule on his throne. And, there shall be a priest on his throne, and the counsel of peace shall be between them both.*

This passage speaks of the King Messiah, who will "build the temple" and "rule on his throne," and the Priest Messiah would be beside him. Further, because we are told that "a counsel of peace shall be between them both," we know that they would be using the same principles to govern.

Zechariah does not imply that the King Messiah would be greater than the Priest Messiah. Other ancient documents such as, the Testament of Levi in the Dead Sea Scrolls, seem to indicate that the priest will be wiser and that the king will be more visible and assertive. Zechariah does not imply that they will be alive at the same time. The Priest could create the wisdom that the King administers later, which would be a logical progression.

In Jewish eschatology, the Priest Messiah is known as "Messiah ben Joseph" (Messiah son of Joseph, who was the son of Jacob). The King Messiah has come to be known as "Messiah ben David" (Messiah son of David). The phrase "son of" does not necessarily imply genetic lineage. It could also mean that one has inherited the spirit, charisma or character of someone who lived previously.

The Priest and King Traditions in the Bible

Let us explore why the Priest Messiah is called "son of Joseph."

Joseph was a mystic, psychic and a wise advisor to the Pharaoh of Egypt. He was the great, great grandson of Abraham, who God later named, "Abraham."

Abram left the Way of Religion in Ur and followed the Way of Wisdom, the Way of soul-knowing. God promised Abram that his decedents would be led into a land of abundance:

> *Now the Lord said to Abram, "Go from your country and your kindred and your father's house to the land that I will show you. And I will make of you a great nation, and I will bless you, and make your name great, so that you will be a blessing. I will bless those who bless you, and him who curses you, I will curse; and by you all the families of the earth shall bless themselves. (Genesis 12: 1-3).*

Abram departed for the land, which has come to be called "the Promised Land," and in the Gospel of Thomas, "the kingdom."

In Thomas, Jesus shows how this passage is fulfilled by anyone when he encounters a wise lion. If the person listens to the lion, he is blessed. If he does not, he is cursed. Thus, Thomas tells us that in order to be the kingdom, one must grow in wisdom by soul-sensing what God is telling him.

A few years later, Abram soul-hears the following:

> *When Abram was ninety-nine years old, the Lord appeared to Abram, and said to him, "I am God Almighty; walk before me, and be blameless. And I will make my covenant between me and you, and will multiply you exceedingly."*

> *Then Abram fell on his face; and God said to him, "Behold, my covenant is with you, and you shall be the father of a multitude of nations. No longer shall your name be Abram (exalted father), but your name shall be Abraham (father of a multitude); for I have made you the father of a multitude of nations. I will make you exceedingly fruitful; and I will make nations of you, and kings shall come forth from you. And I will establish my covenant between me and you and your descendants after you throughout their generations for an everlasting covenant, to be God to you and to your descendants after you. And I will give to you, and to your descendants after you, the land of your sojourning's, all the land of Canaan, for an everlasting possession; and I will be their God." (Genesis 17: 1-8).*

The word "descendent" refers to those who live as Abraham lived, not those who are genetically related to him. Today, those around the world who have left the Way of Religion to follow the Way of Wisdom are the descendants of Abraham. The degree to which they have done so is the degree to which they have entered the Promised Land. In contrast, those who may be genetically related to Abraham and live on the Way of Religion are not the descendants of which God spoke, and have been denied entry into the Promised Land.

Abraham had a son by the name of Isaac. Genesis does not describe him as living in a close relationship with God through soul-knowing as his father did.

Isaac had many sons, one of whom was Jacob. One day Jacob had his first major encounter with God:

> *And Jacob was left alone; and a man wrestled with him until the breaking of the day. When the man saw that he did not prevail against Jacob, he touched the hollow of his thigh; and Jacob's thigh was put out of joint as he wrestled with him. Then he said, "Let me go, for the day is breaking." But Jacob said, "I will not let you go, unless you bless me." And he said to him, "What is your name?" And he said, "Jacob." Then he said, "Your name shall no more be called Jacob, but "Israel," for you have striven with God and with men, and have prevailed." (Genesis 32: 24-28)*

This is the first mention of "Israel" in the Bible. The name means, "one who wrestled with God."

Israel struggled in his relationship with God and finally conquered himself, spending his life letting God lead him through soul-knowing. He did what everyone must do when he leaves the Way of Religion—he fought those parts of himself that prevented him from leaving the world and its religions. While his mind told him to be faithful to authorities, his soul demanded that he follow divine guidance. When he made the wise choice, deciding to live in oneness with God through soul-knowing, he was given his new name. His descendants who live on the Way of Wisdom are Israelites—those who wrestle daily with God and evolve on the Way of Wisdom.

God changed the names of Abraham and Israel, but not Isaac. People today consider Abraham, Isaac and Israel to be the Patriarchs of the Israelites; however, only two of them qualify. The names of Abraham and Jacob were changed after they chose to travel the Way of Wisdom. The fact that God did not change Isaac's name tells us that he remained on the Way of Religion. Thus, Abraham and Israel are the Patriarchs of the Israelites, and Isaac is a Patriarch of the people living among the Israelites, who call themselves Israelites; however, we will see their true identities emerge as this story unfolds.

Israel had twelve sons and at least one daughter. Israel's favorite was Joseph, which tells us that, of the twelve, only one was following the Way of Wisdom.

Because Israel gave Joseph a "coat of many colors," his brothers became jealous, and the oldest brother sold Joseph to traders going to Egypt. That is how Joseph, a type of priest, became the advisor to the Pharaoh. His descendants became the Israelites enslaved in Egypt.

Two of Joseph's descendants were Moses and Aaron. Moses became the reluctant leader who led the Israelites out of Egypt. He was advised by his brother, Aaron. Because Moses found Aaron to be so wise, he anointed him as the first of a line of Priests (Lev. 6:22). Many consider Aaron to be the first Messiah.

Moses, who heard the voice of God, but ruled his people with an iron fist, was never permitted to lead his people out of the wilderness (symbolic of the *process* out of the Way of Religion) into the Promised Land. This tells us that Moses was a Way of Religion leader. When Moses died, Joshua, a leader on the Way of Wisdom, divided the Jordan River (symbolic of the boundary between the Way of Religion and the Way of Wisdom) and led his people into Canaan, the Promised Land.

For over 200 years, the Israelites lived without a king. To resolve disputes, they went to very wise people, called "Judges."

Otherwise, each person was his own leader in oneness with God. We are told in Judges 21:25:

> *In those days there was no king in Israel; every man did what was right in his own eyes.*

As we saw in Thomas, Jesus expressed the same principle for the Way of Wisdom, which might be expressed as: listen to divine guidance through soul-knowing and love-guard all. In this Way, one does and thinks as he is guided by God; however, all within the limits of love-guarding.

We learn in the Book of Samuel that the Way of Wisdom was followed fairly well until Samuel, a leading Judge, appointed his sons as Judges. In 1 Sam 8: 4-20 we learn how the Israelites made a fateful choice that still affects us today.

> *Then all the elders of Israel gathered together and came to Samuel at Ramah, and said to him, "Behold, you are old and your sons do not walk in your ways; now appoint for us a king to govern us like all the nations."*
>
> *But the thing displeased Samuel when they said, "Give us a king to govern us." And Samuel prayed to the Lord.*
>
> *And the Lord said to Samuel, "Hearken to the voice of the people in all that they say to you; for they have not rejected you, but they have rejected me from being king over them. According to all the deeds which they have done to me, from the day I brought them up out of Egypt even to this day, forsaking me and serving other gods, so they are also doing to you. Now then, hearken to their voice; only, you shall solemnly warn them, and show them the ways of the king who shall reign over them."*

So Samuel told all the words of the Lord to the people who were asking a king from him. He said, "These will be the ways of the king who will reign over you...He will take the tenth of your flocks, and you shall be his slaves. And in that day you will cry out because of your king, whom you have chosen for yourselves; but the Lord will not answer you in that day."

But the people refused to listen to the voice of Samuel; and they said, "No! But we will have a king over us, that we also may be like all the nations, and that our king may govern us."

"Now appoint for us a king to govern us like all the nations. But the request displeased Samuel when they said, "Give us a king to govern us."

The elders asked to be ruled by a king rather than following divine guidance. Samuel resisted because they were choosing the Way of Religion.

"And the Lord said to Samuel, "Hearken to the voice of the people in all that they say to you; for they have not rejected you, but they have rejected Me from being king over them."

The people had a choice between being ruled by a king, or by God.

"So Samuel told all the words of the Lord to the people who were asking a king from him. He said, 'These will be the ways of the king who will reign over you...He will take the tenth of your flocks, and you shall be his slaves. And in that day you will cry out because of your king, whom you have chosen for yourselves; but the Lord will not answer you in that day.'"

Samuel returns to the elders and warns them. He tells them that the king will make them tithe and be his slaves. They will cry out in pain to God, and that One will not answer them. As we know, for 2700 years since then, people have cried out to God for relief from their rulers, and have found only more inner conflict and conflict between people and nations.

The first king was Saul, who could not control the tension between those on the two Ways. Eventually, he was killed and Samuel anointed David as king. To unite the people, David established what we now know as Judaism, a Way of Religion. He demanded that they follow his ways of worshiping God, his laws, and his priests, who manipulated the people into obeying him by telling them that by doing so, they were obeying God. Before David died, he began preparing to build the first temple. David may have also been the one who composed the Torah laws and had them inserted into the story of Moses, to make it appear as if God proclaimed the laws through Moses. They then became the laws of his kingdom.

His son, Solomon, became the next king, finished the temple, and continued enforcing David's Way of Religion. As a result, the kingdom of David became divided. Most of the true Israelites, those on the Way of Wisdom, chose to live in the north. Those on the Way of Religion came to reside largely in the south in Judea, near the Temple in Jerusalem. Because of that, they came to be called "Jews." Those in the north were called, "Israelites."

Eventually, Assyria conquered the Israelites and they were scattered to various parts of the Assyrian empire, from which they migrated to many countries. They have come to be called the "lost tribes."

The Role of the Priest Messiah

Old Testament prophets foretold that one of the coming Messiahs would gather the scattered Israelites. We read in Jeremiah 31:

> *Hear the word of the Lord, O nations, and declare it in the coastlands afar off; say, "He who scattered Israel will gather him, and will keep him as a shepherd keeps his flock" (Jer. 31:10).*

> *There is hope for your future, says the Lord,
> and your children shall come back to their own
> country (Jer. 31:17).*

"He who scattered Israel will gather them and keep them as a shepherd keeps his flock." He who scattered the followers of Jacob will empower a Messiah to teach them.

"And your children shall come back to their own country." And those Israelites on the Way of Wisdom will return to their land, which Jesus calls a "place" and "the kingdom."

People following the Way of Religion have interpreted these passages to mean that Jews will return to the country Israel, which happened in 1948. Another interpretation is that those all over the world on the Way of Wisdom will become one in that place within, in oneness with "He Who Lives." That will happen when a Priest Messiah teaches them the Way of Wisdom.

Jeremiah explains the role of the Priest Messiah further in 31:33-34:

> *But this is the covenant which I will make with
> the house of Israel after those days, says the Lord:
> I will put my law within them, and I will write
> it upon their hearts; and I will be their God, and
> they shall be my people. And no longer shall each
> man teach his neighbor and each his brother,
> saying, 'Know the Lord,' for they shall all know
> me, from the least of them to the greatest, says the
> Lord; for I will forgive their iniquity, and I will
> remember their sin no more (Jer. 31: 33-34).*

"But this is the covenant which I will make with the house of Israel." The word "house" means "family," "family and friends," and "descendants." Thus, Jeremiah predicts that there will be a new covenant (promise) to those on the Way of Wisdom.

"I will put my law within them, and I will write it upon their hearts; and I will be their God, and they shall be my people." A Priest Messiah will teach people the natural laws of God. Those laws will be recognized in their "hearts." Religious authorities will no longer be their Gods. Instead, God who guides them through soul-knowing will be their King.

Conclusion: The Priest Messiah will teach the people of the world the Way of Wisdom.

The Role of the King Messiah

The King Messiah will implement the Priest Messiah's gospel. We read that in Ezekiel 37: 21-28

> *Thus says the Lord God: "Behold, I will take the people of Israel from the nations among which they have gone, and will gather them from all sides, and bring them to their own land; and I will make them one nation in the land, upon the mountains of Israel.*
>
> *And one king shall be king over them all; and they shall be no longer two nations, and no longer divided into two kingdoms.*
>
> *They shall not defile themselves any more with their idols and their detestable things, or with any of their transgressions; but I will save them from all the back-slidings in which they have sinned, and will cleanse them; and they shall be my people, and I will be their God.*
>
> *My servant David will be king over them, and they will all have one shepherd. They will follow my laws and be careful to keep my decrees.*
>
> *They will live in the land I gave to my servant Jacob, the land where your ancestors lived. They*

and their children and their children's children will live there forever, and David my servant will be their prince forever.

I will make a covenant of peace with them; it will be an everlasting covenant.

I will establish them and increase their numbers, and I will put my sanctuary among them forever. My dwelling place will be with them; I will be their God, and they will be my people.

Then the nations will know that I the Lord make Israel holy, when my sanctuary is among them forever."

"Behold, I will take the people of Israel from the nations among which they have gone, and will gather them from all sides, and bring them to their own land; and I will make them one nation in the land, upon the mountains of Israel." The King Messiah will teach everyone living all over the world a common Way of Wisdom. In doing so, he will "bring them to their own land," the Promised Land, which Jesus calls "the kingdom." It is within each person and it unites them into "one nation." Further, that Messiah will put that nation "upon the mountains of Israel," that is, those people will become mountains on Israel's (Jacob's) Way of Wisdom.

"And one king shall be king over them all."

Just as Joseph was the teacher of the Pharaoh, and Aaron was the teacher of Moses, and Samuel taught King David, the Priest Messiah will educate the King Messiah. It will be the job of the King Messiah to defend and promote the gospel of the Priest Messiah.

"And they shall be no longer two nations, and no longer divided into two kingdoms." The King Messiah will do the opposite of King David, who forced people following the Way of Wisdom to adopt his Way of Religion. The King Messiah will instead disrupt the Ways of Religion of the world, expose the harm they cause, and lead people onto the Way of Wisdom that the Priest Messiah has preached. As Ezekiel says so powerfully:

"They (those on the Way of Religion) shall not defile themselves any more with their idols (theology and clergy), and their detestable things (so-called sacred garments, utensils, and buildings), or with any of their transgressions (for example, discrimination against and persecution of women, gays and people of different faiths); but I will save them from all the backslidings (on the Ways of Religion) in which they have sinned, and will cleanse them; and they shall be my people, and I will be their God (everyone will become one on God's Way). "

"My servant David will be king over them, and they will all have one shepherd. They will follow my laws and be careful to keep my decrees."

The King Messiah will be the "one shepherd." There will no longer be different religions with different leaders. Instead, they will be governed by God's natural laws.

"They will live in the land I gave to my servant Jacob, the land where your ancestors lived. They and their children and their children's children will live there forever, and David my servant will be their prince forever." They will live in the Promised Land, that is, in the kingdom—the same one in which Jacob and your ancestors on the Way of Wisdom lived—this time forever.

"I will make a covenant of peace with them; it will be an everlasting covenant." I will ensure that there will be no more conflict within or between those on the Way of Wisdom.

"I will establish them and increase their numbers, and I will put my sanctuary among them forever. My dwelling place will be with them; I will be their God, and they will be my people." I will ensure that the number of people on the Way of Wisdom increase. Further, I will establish my temple in the heart of each of them forever. I will be with them, at the center of their every thought and action.

"Then, the nations will know that I the Lord make Israel holy, when my sanctuary is among them forever." Then, those on the Way of Religion will know that I, the Lord, make the Israelites (those on the Way of Wisdom) holy. Everyone will see me as the center of their lives.

Ezekiel emphasized that the Messiah King would bring peace. However, according to Daniel, initially the King will bring war:

> *In the time of those kings, the God of heaven will set up a kingdom that will never be destroyed, nor will it be left to another people. It will crush all those kingdoms and bring them to an end, but it will itself endure forever (Daniel 2:44).*

"In the time of those kings." When the Messiah comes, there will be many kings over many Ways of Religion. All of them will be indoctrinators; all of them will be declaring their Ways as the truth; all of them will be distorting and hiding information to manipulate their constituents.

"The God of heaven will set up a kingdom that will never be destroyed, nor will it be left to another people." God, who is heavenly wise and alive, will establish his divine way of being in the hearts of many. Those people will unite and become a ruling force in the world against all of the different Ways of Religion. Once established, the worldwide kingdom of the Way of Wisdom will rule forever.

In other words, humankind has not clearly seen the difference between the Ways of Religion and the Way of Wisdom. Once that has been articulated, promoted, and embraced by enough people, humankind will see living examples of an alternative to conflict. No more will they be confused about how to resolve their inner anxieties and worries. No longer will they be fighting to establish their truth and ego over others. No more will they be slaves to religious kings. Instead, they will transform their fears into love daily, empower others to find their own truths, and serve one King that they will sense through soul-knowing.

Once a kingdom of enough people on the Way of Wisdom becomes visible, everyone will see and remember. Thus, those people (Kings) on the Way of Religion will not be attractive any longer to seekers.

"It will crush all those kingdoms and bring them to an end, but it will itself endure forever." Initially, the Way of Religion kings will resist; however, they will eventually be crushed by lion-children, whose legacy will endure forever.

Was Jesus the Messiah?

As we saw above, the Old Testament Prophets predicted two Messiahs. Jesus was the Priest Messiah.

The King Messiah has not appeared—unless it is the Gospel of Thomas that was probably authored by Jesus. If the King Messiah is a person, he will arrive riding the horse of divine power with the Gospels of Mark and Thomas in his saddle bag. In either case, the Book of Revelations (Rev 6:2, 19:11,14) will be fulfilled:

Behold a white horse!

And
its rider
had a bow,

And a crown
was given to him,

And
he
went out conquering
to conquer.

And
the armies of heaven,
followed him
on white horses,

They
arrayed in fine linen
white and pure.

Rev 6:2, 19:11,14

White Horse = Heavenly Power
Rider = Second Coming of the Messiah
Armies = Those on the Messiah's Way

ACKNOWLEDGEMENTS

An author's name is on the front of the book. He does do the bulk of the work; however, in most cases, and this is one, he could not have done it without the support of others.

This book is the fruit of 15 years of idea hoeing, planting, weeding, pruning, and harvesting. I worked the first five years alone in a cabin in the desert outside Santa Fe, New Mexico. I may have gone crazy and given up if it were not for three people: my brother Don continued to check in on me from New York, Charlie Leavitt provided encouragement and offered me training gigs, and Joe Rook, my first editor, reviewed and revised every idea and page. Their almost weekly emails and calls were a lifeline to reality.

I then, moved to Mexico and met my wife. She has been largely supportive for 9 years without a clue about what I was doing.

Concerned about her and the kids, I rushed out a book with incomplete style and content ideas. During that process, a number of people provided support:

My editor, Bruce Klippenstein and his wife Linda.

Tom Novak with the illustrations and cover.

My friend Marvin Baker who also helped us move to Guanajuato and survive there,

Jeff Chase and Gwen Boucher, both of whom said, "I believe in you" when I found it difficult to believe in myself,

My former high school buddy, Jack Ewers,

Two former Jesuit buddies, Jack Linn and Norm Betz,

My cousin/sister, Nancy Parzych, the best there is, who kept writing to say that she could not understand why anyone would be interested, but that she was behind me,

My brother Rick,

Raul, a poor but rich man, living high in the mountain village of Terrero, Guanajuato who helped with his friendship, music and anything else that he had,

We then moved on to Punta Banda, BC, Mexico. Generous souls immediately offered us a hand. They included:

Dan Mantz, who, without understanding much, said, "Sounds good, go live in my vacant house near the beach,"

Ed Krause, who helped when one daughter was kidnapped (we got her back),

Will Lynch, who at 80 years old and counting, living by himself in a house without electricity, made sure that we survived,

William Gower, who helped with the book's final production,

And my three wonderful editors,

- Don Talarico, who, as my close friend and sounding board, also established the book's style,
- Brandon Phillips, who did the copyediting, and
- Aundria Warren, who did the final detail editing.

So you see, it took many people to make this revelation of the real Jesus possible.

Made in the USA
San Bernardino, CA
08 January 2017